FREEDOM'S CHILDREN

Young Civil Rights Activists Tell Their Own Stories

ELLEN LEVINE

AN AVON FLARE BOOK

*For my father, Nathan Levine,
and in memory of my mother, Ide Gruber Levine,
both of whom abhorred and fought prejudice,
and took great pleasure in the fact
that their three daughters were
on the March on Washington in 1963.*

Photograph credits

AP/Wide World Photos, p. 111; Birmingham Public Library, Department
of Archives, p. 70; Black Star, © 1961 Charles Moore, p. 93; Magnum
Photos, Inc., © Elliott Erwitt, p. 1; NAACP Public Relations, p. 37; Jim
Peppler, pp. 141, 167; Dan Weiner, courtesy of Sandra Weiner, p. 18

AVON BOOKS
A division of
The Hearst Corporation
1350 Avenue of the Americas
New York, New York 10019

Copyright © 1993 by Ellen Levine
Published by arrangement with G.P. Putnam's Sons
Library of Congress Catalog Card Number: 92–1358
ISBN: 0-380-72114-7

First Avon Flare Printing: January 1994

AVON FLARE TRADEMARK REG. U.S. PAT. OFF. AND IN OTHER COUNTRIES,
MARCA REGISTRADA, HECHO EN U.S.A.

Printed in the U.S.A.

OPM 10 9 8 7 6

Contents

1 The Color Bar: Experiences of Segregation   1

2 The Montgomery Bus Boycott and the
    Beginning of the Movement   18

3 Different Classrooms: Segregation and
    Integration in the Schools   37

4 Sit-ins, Freedom Rides, and Other Protests   70

5 The Children's Crusade   93

6 The Closed Society: Mississippi and
    Freedom Summer   111

7 Bloody Sunday and the Selma Movement   141

Epilogue   167
Chronology   173
Who's Who   180
Acronyms   192

Bibliographical Note   193
Index   195

Photograph Section
between pages 92 and 93.

Preface

Many have asked me how I found people to interview for this book. There are thousands of southern blacks who were young and involved in the civil rights movement during the 1950s and 1960s, but with a few exceptions, they aren't famous. Precisely because of that, I wanted to tell their stories. With all the talk of the importance of "role models," I believe that among the most powerful models for young people today are their heroic counterparts of yesterday—not heroes on pedestals, adult and remote, but kids like themselves who believed that their world could change for the better and undertook the challenge to make the changes.

But how to find these young people? Demonstrations, boycotts, marches, and other forms of public protest were a tangible sign of involvement, and so I began with the major events from 1955 to 1965—the Montgomery Bus Boycott, the Little Rock school integration crisis, the Birmingham protests, Mississippi Summer, Bloody Sunday and the Selma Movement. Before traveling south, I read extensively, and then began telephoning. I called churches, community groups, someone's aunt or cousin, anyone or any group I could find, searching for names of people who were children or teenagers during the movement days.

I called Montgomery, Alabama, telephone information for a listing for Rosa Parks. She wasn't a young person at the time of the bus boycott, but perhaps she could direct me to some who were. I introduced myself to the woman who answered the phone and described the project. She listened patiently and then told me she wasn't "that Rosa Parks," but she wanted to help. She stood up at her church service and asked for names of people who were young and involved at the time of the boycott. She gave me names. Later, when I arrived in Montgomery, Gwen Patton, who tells her story in these pages, was a daily source of information and support.

Because of a casual conversation with Erma Malloy, who was sitting next to me at Howard University's oral archives, I was put in touch with Mildred Tucker, a remarkable woman who lives in Birmingham, Alabama. She called me every day when I was in Birmingham with a list of new people for me to contact.

Friends of mine who had lived and worked in Mississippi during movement days gave me the names of young people they had known. Aviva Futorian, a college friend who had spent a year and a half working first as a Freedom School teacher and then as a SNCC organizer in Mississippi, was extremely helpful. We talked almost daily during my stay in that state. Ben Chaney was most helpful in providing me with additional names. And in the way of these things, one person then led to another.

When I went south to begin interviewing, people were extraordinarily generous and helpful. Every day during the time I was there, someone would say,

"I've been thinking, and I know someone who . . ." And that's how I found most of the people in the book. My only regret is that I haven't been able to include the stories of everyone I talked with.

I have many to thank. First, of course, the people whose voices fill these pages. They spent many long hours talking with me, reliving a past, sharing memories of laughter, adventure, triumph, and sadness.

Others helped in various ways. Some housed me during my travels, or spent time thinking of people for me to contact; lawyer friends checked citations and copied cases for me; others gave me books that were pertinent but not easy to find; family and friends were "just there" for lunch, dinner, and words of encouragement. To all of them I am most beholden: Julie Abraham, Daisy Bates, Velma Bates, Adrienne Bernard, Dori Brenner, Sara Bullard, Larry Davis, Ann Diamond, Marie Foster, Barbara Garson, Judy Hole, Annette Horwitz, Orisis Icarus, Linda Kamm, Ingrid Kindred, Lise Kreps, Susan Kuklin, Ira Landess, Bob Lavelle, Mada Liebman, Leslie McLemore, Jan Meren, Diane Nash, Phyllis Richman, Deborah Sandford, Reverend Fred Shuttlesworth, Frank Sikora, William Singleton, Fanny Watson, Katie Watson, and Roslyn Yasser.

I am also most grateful to David Garrow, who opened his extensive files and flipped his Wheeldex to give me a long list of names to contact. And to Anne Koedt, who read, and reread, and reread the manuscript, always supportive, always insightful.

A special thanks to Frank Leonardo, who performed miracles on my ailing computer.

And finally, my deep gratitude to Refna Wilkin, my editor. Only the space restrictions she has imposed prevent my detailing her many virtues.

Note to the Reader

Most of the text of this book is comprised of the stories the people I interviewed told me over long hours of conversation. To set the context for these oral histories, I have written introductions with background material to each chapter. In a number of instances I have felt it necessary to insert additional background information in the text of an interview. This material is printed in italics.

Introduction

This book is about thirty young African Americans—children and teenagers—who tell in their own words of their involvement in the civil rights movement of the 1950s and 1960s. Uncluttered by concerns of power or fame, they had the simplest and clearest of political urges, the impulse for freedom.

They grew up in cities and towns in Alabama, Mississippi, and Arkansas. And there were thousands more like them throughout the South. But wherever their homes, they had a common knowledge and shared experience of segregation, its rules, its humiliations, and its dangers.

From Montgomery, Alabama, to Itta Bena, Mississippi, there was little difference, for example, in the insulting tones of the white insurance man who, on his weekly collection visits to black homes, invariably called older black persons by their first names, while he expected to be addressed as "Mister."

Throughout the South the "colored" water fountain was more than an abstract symbol of segregation. It was for many a daily slap in the face. The city bus signs for a "colored" section that sent black people to the back, or forced them to stand over empty "white only" seats, were a constant source of anger and frustration.

Black children throughout the South shared a history that included the 1955 murder of fourteen-year-old Emmett Till, killed for allegedly having talked "improperly" to a white woman in a small-town store in Mississippi. He "had broken that code," one young Mississippian says in these pages. And he died for it.

They shared the triumph of the Montgomery Bus Boycott, when thousands of blacks stayed off the city buses for over a year to protest segregation. They all were aware of the landmark school desegregation decision in 1954, *Brown v. Board of Education of Topeka*, in which the United States Supreme Court declared school segregation unconstitutional. And they all knew of the Little Rock Nine, the black high school students who in 1957 faced off a hysterical white community and, under the eyes and guns of U.S. troops, finished out the school year.

No matter where they came from, they knew of the Birmingham, Alabama, church bombing in 1963, in which four young black girls were killed. Often their parents tried to stop their involvement by reminding them of the Birmingham tragedy, but they weren't deterred. And they all knew of "Bloody Sunday" and the subsequent Selma-to-Montgomery march that triggered the passage of the landmark Voting Rights Act of 1965.

This book is not a traditional history of the civil rights movement. Rather it is a collection of individual histories that together create a larger picture. Although beatings, arrests, and death were an intrinsic part of the story of the movement, these are not tales of sadness and despair. To the contrary, the young people in these pages speak of a pride, a confidence, a joy at being part of something they knew was right.

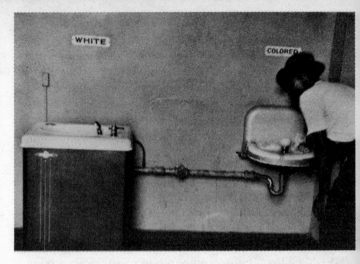

Separate water fountains for whites and coloreds.

1. The Color Bar: Experiences of Segregation

Segregation was not abstract to black people living in the South; it was about everyday life. It touched every corner of southern existence imaginable—movie theaters, hospitals, libraries, taxicabs, restaurants, schools, jobs, buses, stores, parks, water fountains, churches, cemeteries.

In one Alabama city, the public library wouldn't have children's books that showed black and white rabbits together. In another city, blacks and whites were forbidden to play checkers with each other in public places. In South Carolina, white and black cotton mill workers weren't permitted to look out the same window. In Oklahoma, telephone booths were segregated. However absurd these rules may seem today, they were meant to discriminate against and demean black people.

Some segregationists didn't stop with rules that favored whites. They supported the use of violence against blacks. Even young black children knew about the Ku Klux Klan and other white supremacist groups. They knew that blacks were beaten, arrested, terrorized, even murdered, with little or no recourse under the law. They knew that white judges often dismissed cases brought by blacks. They knew that if a case did go to trial, all-white juries rarely would convict a white for a crime against a black.

The following stories, some long, some short, re-create the segregated world as it was for young black people in the 1950s and 1960s. The children who tell their stories in this book had an immediate and palpable sense of things. They perceived the specific humiliation for exactly what it was and what was meant by it. They understood what was happening when they were given stale cookies, or sent to a separate table to eat, or heard their elders saying "Yessir" and "No sir" to white people decades younger than they were.

All of these stories reveal the extent and the meanness of bigotry. Read together, they are a patchwork of anger, humor, pain, hope, and most of all, courage.

■□

BEN CHANEY—MERIDIAN, MISSISSIPPI

We lived across the street from a white family. From my side of the street on, it was the black community, and from their side of the street, it was the white community. Up until the time I was about ten years old, I always played with those white kids. But once I became ten, their parents came straight out and told me they didn't want me playing with their kids no more. Their mama told them they were better than I was, and told me I couldn't associate with her son, and I had to call him "Mister." And the kids themselves adopted that attitude.

GWENDOLYN PATTON—
MONTGOMERY, ALABAMA

Gwen Patton grew up in Detroit, Michigan. She spent summers with relatives in Montgomery until she moved there at age sixteen.

There was this peculiar thing with my birth. About six weeks before my mother bore me, her brother was shot by the police in Montgomery, and it had civil rights overtones. My family has always felt that that incident impacted on my mother so much that I was born a civil rights worker. I was very, very independent, and I was fierce about my freedom.

I loved the South as a child. I had a whole group of friends and cousins down here. I remember one summer specifically. After Sunday school and church, my brother, my first cousin Al, and myself would ride the bus. That was a Sunday treat. We would ride for fifteen cents all the way down to the end of the line and then ride it back. I was nine and the oldest, and this particular Sunday I decided that we would stop and buy an ice-cream cone downtown.

At that time you had soda fountains, which was a big thing in my childhood. We also went to get some water. You paid three cents for this little cone-shaped paper cup, and I proceeded to sit down. This lady behind the counter told me I couldn't do that. I sensed something was wrong. She didn't call me any names or anything, but I sensed that it was because I was black. So I poured my cup of water on the counter, instructing my brother and my cousin to do likewise. The people in the store were absolutely shocked. We stormed out, got on the bus, and went home. I was outraged.

That was our first protest and boycott. When I came home and told my grandmother, she was very calm. I don't remember her at all becoming excited or lecturing or anything. But I do recall that I never was allowed to ride the bus again.

JAMES ROBERSON—BIRMINGHAM, ALABAMA

My mother wanted to leave Alabama. She could not take the hostility and the racial problems. My dad was a railroad man, and he tried to get transferred to Cincinnati. While he was waiting, my mom packed us up and we moved. I was about ten or eleven. In Cincinnati there weren't open, blatant racial differences. I talked as a black southerner, so in school I was nicknamed "Alabama." But when I went to the board and could outdo the other kids academically, they began to accept me.

When my dad could not get transferred, we came back. On the way, the train stopped in a little town in northern Alabama called Decatur. I wanted something to eat, so I got off. I wasn't thinking about being black. I went in the front door of the train station. Suddenly everything stopped. A lady said, "Get out of here, nigger! You get out of here!" I was shocked. I ran out and got back on the train. I told my mom what had happened. She said, "Baby, you back down South."

When that happened, it dawned on me that the lady didn't know if I was a good child, or a bad child, or a loving son, or an angel. Just because I was brown and had black hair, I could not eat there.

The green sign on the Birmingham city buses was one of the most powerful pieces of wood in the city. It was about the size of a shoe box and fit into the holes on the back of the bus seats. On one side of the board it said "Colored, do not sit beyond this board." The bus driver had the authority to move that green board in any direction he wanted to at any time.

To give you an example, the bus might be headed for Collegeville in North Birmingham, where blacks lived. When the maids and chauffeurs and street sweepers—those were the jobs for blacks in those days—would get on the bus, they'd all be seated. In another mile, ten whites might get on. The driver would get the green board, move it, and the blacks would have to get up. A seventy-year-old black person might have to move for a six-year-old white child.

A group of us formed a little club called the Eagles. When we would get on the buses, I would take the green sign and move it up or throw it away. I was a teenager, and that was my way of fighting the system.

Sometimes we would defy the green board. We would sit right behind the bus driver. You really had to imagine the driver as a cobra snake or a vicious dog, and you're treading on his territory. You know that if you move close to him, he's going to strike you. The driver would say, "All right, you niggers got to get up."

We'd say, "You talking to us?" There were guys who were like conductors and drove black plain cars. The bus driver would get off and call one of those guys. He would come on and say, "Get off or we're gonna call the law."

"So call them," we said. When he'd go to call, we'd get off the bus and disappear.

James attended Bethel Baptist Church where Reverend Fred Shuttlesworth organized some of the earliest civil rights demonstrations in the 1950s. In December 1956, a group led by Reverend Shuttlesworth was arrested for sitting in the "white" section on a Birmingham city bus. Shortly thereafter, on Christmas night, the Bethel Baptist Church parsonage was bombed. James was thirteen years old at the time.

I was home in bed. The explosion was so powerful, I thought the world was coming to an end. The vibration was enormous—if you can imagine fifty times as much thunder as you normally hear. My daddy jumped up and he ran through the house to check on us. He said, "There's been a bomb!" I ran to the front. My mother used to collect little ceramic things. The explosion had knocked all that down and everything was broken. The windows were out.

I looked across to the church. The electric wires were still flashing from the explosion. You could smell burnt rags and gunpowder. People were screaming. The parsonage had collapsed on one side. My father and Mr. Revis rushed over. Reverend was in his bedroom, which was against the outer wall of the parsonage. Between that outer wall and the church was a three-foot walkway. They had put the bomb in that walkway right next to the bedroom wall. A rafter, one of those big ones, went right through the bed. Daddy was saying he thought Reverend was dead. If he had been in that bed when the beam came through, he would have been. But the explosion had thrown Reverend out of bed.

Reverend got up and came out. He had on an old, long coat, one of those topcoats preachers wear. He did not have a mark on his body, not a drop of blood. That dynamite had blown windows out a mile or more away, but he had no deafness from the sound. He had nothing physically wrong with him. Think about it. The police said eight to eighteen sticks of dynamite went off within three feet of this man's head. He's not deaf, he's not blind, he's not crippled, he's not bleeding. That really made me think he had to be Godsent.

People had come from blocks around to see what had happened. They had sawed-off shotguns and pistols. Any white man who had gone through there probably would have been hurt. The Reverend stood in the middle of this rubble and talked about nonviolence. He said, "Go home! Put the guns away!" I never will forget him singling out one man. "You all get him and take him home. He's got a gun. We're not going to be violent. We don't want that. This is not gonna turn us around." In the middle of that house leaning over, the sparking electric wires, the police on their way, people gathered with guns and hostility, he gave a sermon.

FRED SHUTTLESWORTH, JR.—
BIRMINGHAM, ALABAMA

Fred Shuttlesworth, Jr. was ten years old at the time of the Christmas bombing of his home.

It was about 9:30 or 10 o'clock at night. My father was in the bedroom talking with Mr. Robinson. Usually I was sitting next to Ricky watching television, but that time I was in the dining room. I was wearing my red football uniform that I had gotten that day. All of a sudden, BOOM! It was just like a war zone.

When I saw all that dust and stuff in the air, I knew that somebody had actually tried to kill us. There was this big question mark. Why would anyone want to do something like this to me and us?

Then the fear came. I began to stutter. I didn't know why at the time. It was rough because you don't understand what is happening to you. Some folks are aggressive; some folks are passive and go into a shell. I was neither. I just stuttered every once in a while.

My uncle and aunt kept us for that year while the house was being rebuilt. He more than anybody else gave me things to read and encouraged me to express myself. I don't stutter now. But then it was the fear coming out physically.

ROY DEBERRY—HOLLY SPRINGS, MISSISSIPPI

I remember one incident when I was at my grandmother's. I was about five or six. She had a Singer sewing machine without the electricity. She would ask me to get down on the floor and pedal the thing for her. We were out in the yard and an old white man who was poor was coming up. My grandmother was preparing food, so it was obvious that she was going to give him some. I said, "Grandma, what does this cracker want?"

She said, "You don't do that. You don't call someone a 'cracker.' This man wants some food. He's hungry." I remember her feeding him, and that was really the first time I saw a white person come to our house for food. She also used that as an opportunity to teach me something. People are people, even though they're not always good people.

Growing up I knew the rules. It was clear. You went to the courthouse and there was the "colored" bathroom and "white." You saw the signs. I don't think we had a public water fountain in Holly Springs except at the courthouse. But you see, Mr. Armstead, who was black, had his store, and so when we wanted water, we could just drink there.

I didn't experience it, but I heard my grandfather and my father say that generally if there was a white person on the sidewalk, you actually got off to let them pass. You also could not look at a white woman. I remember my mother telling us certain things. She never just came out and said, "Don't you all look at a white woman," but it was kind of understood that you tried to avoid as much eye contact as possible.

Of course I heard about Emmett Till in 1955. Even at age seven it was shocking. We knew that a fourteen-year-old boy had been killed for allegedly whistling at a white woman. We knew that was one of those codes, and that he was killed because he had broken that code. We knew that was evil, and we knew the evil could happen again.

I think that was a watershed. Not only was Emmett Till killed, but there was almost an absolute cover-up. The system decided to completely close and say we're not going to see justice done here.

THELMA EUBANKS—MCCOMB, MISSISSIPPI

I first heard of the movement through mass meetings at the church. At the mass meeting they talked about all of the things that were going on around here. The church bombings had started at that time. I think sixteen black churches got bombed around here. They never tried anybody for it, but we knew the Klan was doing it. Later on they tried to bomb our church, but the gunpowder wouldn't go off. That's when the blacks got the neighborhood watch committee. Three or four of the church members would stay up with rifles, watching.

They burned crosses. I saw one. It was burned on this lady's yard one night. She was a black schoolteacher. She didn't have anything to do with the movement, but I guess they put it up there because it was high ground, and everybody could see it. White folks got some funny religion around here. They really do, when it comes to blacks. I guess they think ain't nobody going to heaven except white folks.

But the cross burning didn't make me afraid. I've never been afraid once I got involved. I didn't think about being afraid. A lot of people were afraid, I guess, that people would try to burn their houses down. I don't know why I wasn't afraid. Maybe I didn't have sense enough to be.

Blacks used to be slaves, and slavery was bad down in this part of the country. My grandparents were sharecroppers. They stayed on the white folks' place. So they had to do what they said to do. My grandmama used to tell me stories. Her and my grandfather were on wagons and horses then. They could be riding through Liberty or Amite County, and if a white man wanted her, she got on the back of that wagon with him, and my grandfather dared not turn around. When they got through with her, she just got back up there and sat beside him and kept going.

JUDY TARVER—FAIRFIELD, ALABAMA

I had a white doll with blond hair. They probably didn't make a black doll. And then a lot of our people at that time were conditioned to think that maybe the lighter-skinned blacks were somehow superior to the darker. Black was not a popular word. It was a stigma if you were dark-skinned. Oh, you better not call anybody black! That was a fighting word amongst our own people until the sixties. Then it changed and got to be the thing. I felt real good about that change.

Whenever you would hear whites speak, all you ever heard them say was "nigras." How could they go to church on Sunday and have these kind of feelings? We'd pass their churches. They would be full of cars everywhere. When I'd see them, I'd say, "What are they even talking about in there?" It looked like they were always out in droves at church. And yet they weren't any nicer to their fellow man.

Myrna Carter—birmingham, alabama

My grandmother was very, very outspoken. She was a great inspiration because she was not afraid of white people. And I just loved that. We called her Big Chief White Cloud. She had a lot of Indian in her. I never will forget the day the insurance man came to the house and made the mistake of calling her "Auntie." She said, "Do you have a black Auntie? I'm not your Auntie, so don't you call me Auntie no more." I was in elementary school when that happened.

During the fifties, freedom was something that we only read about. It was a fantasy, in a sense. We felt that being free was being able to go where you wanted to go, do what you wanted to do, without fear. When we traveled, we could not use the restrooms even at service stations. We had to stop on the side of the highway. Daddy would always let the doors stay open, and that would be like a cover to protect us from the oncoming cars.

We couldn't take advantage of things we saw other people doing. If we were in a store first and some white came in, they would stop waiting on us. We would have to wait, and we could not interrupt. I remember something that happened once in either Loveman's or Pitzitz, where they have drawers with hats. This salesperson was showing some white people hats. Another white lady began to open the drawers and look at hats. A black lady standing there thought that while she was waiting she could do the same thing. So she opened the drawers. The saleslady acted like she had committed a crime. She told her, "You don't go in those drawers. You wait until I get to you!" That stayed with me a long time. I was about ten or eleven when that happened, and I could not understand it.

When I was about the same age, I used to go to Silver's five-and-ten-cent store. I loved sugar wafers. They had strawberry, chocolate, and vanilla ones sitting in a glass case on the counter. I was showing the saleslady what I wanted, but I noticed she was not getting them out from the case where I could see them. I asked her where they were from. All she said was, "I'm getting these cookies for you. Do you want them?"

I found out they were the old cookies they had taken out and replaced with fresh ones. She was giving me these old ones from a box underneath. She truly was mean. I told her I did not want them. Whenever I would go in Silver's again, she would always recognize my face. She knew I was the one who refused to take those cookies. When I went back, I would not let her wait on me.

PAT SHUTTLESWORTH—
BIRMINGHAM, ALABAMA

I remember getting out of high school early one day. I was about fourteen. Some of my girlfriends and I went downtown to go to the movies. We decided to get hot dogs, hamburgers, and pop before we got to the theater because in the theater we didn't get the same caliber of goods as white people got. There were about fifteen or twenty of us, and we went in this restaurant. Most of us ordered two hot dogs, or a hot dog and a hamburger, and the big 16-ounce pops. You know how you splurge your allowance when you're with your friends.

The man opened all the bottles. When he fixed everything, we asked him where we could sit to eat. He said, "Oh, you can't sit in here."

I said, "We can't? After buying all this food, we can't sit in here and eat it? Well then, we don't need it." He used a couple of choice words, saying that we had to buy it.

I said, "I don't have to buy anything. I'm hungry, but I can go where I can be accommodated the way I want to be accommodated."

"What am I going to do with this food?" he said.

"Whatever you want to do with it. We don't want it." And we turned around and left.

RICKY SHUTTLESWORTH—
BIRMINGHAM, ALABAMA

I thought a lot about ending segregation because Daddy was so involved, and we got so many threats and telephone calls. I remember I used to think that if I had one wish, it would be that everybody would be blind. Then nobody would know what color anything was.

LARRY RUSSELL—BIRMINGHAM, ALABAMA

When I was a real small kid, it was just the delight of your heart to go to town on Saturday. My mother used to take me to this store called J. J. Newberry. On the main floor was the snack bar. It was a "white only" snack bar. Down in the basement in the back of the store in a corner was where coloreds ate. It didn't have half the variety of what was upstairs. When you'd pass through the main floor, the aroma from the "white only" snack bar was just terrific.

When I was twelve or thirteen, I'd go to Newberry's with friends. They had one water fountain for whites, and one for us. I used to think, What's the difference between colored water and white water? What does white water taste like? I couldn't wait to catch the drop on somebody to find out. My friend Joe and I went in there many nights and waited and waited until it was time for the store to close. They were busy trying to get people out, and we'd get us a sip of "white" water. It tasted no different. Water was water. The only thing different was with the black one you practically had to put your mouth on the thing to drink out of it. On the white side, they hardly had to bend over. Their water came up so free. This was mystifying.

After my father's regular work shift, he would do odd jobs for white folks. There was this nurse that Daddy worked for. When her name came up in our house, everybody stopped. If she called and said she needed Daddy to come over and knock the roof off the house, he'd get up out of his sleep to do it.

She and her sister lived together. One Saturday she wanted somebody to help do some housework. I went to do mopping. She paid nicely. She was one of the head nurses at the hospital. I got there and started to work. They were going to eat, and they asked me if I wanted something. Naturally, first I said no. They insisted. "We cooked more than we can eat. Why don't you come on and eat with us?" They were eating hot dogs. I really wanted to get through and get home, but since they were insisting, and I'd always been taught by my folks to be polite, I said, "Well, in that case, I'd be happy to."

They were both sitting at the table. They had the meal all prepared. She told me, "Wash your hands and come on in." I thought that was a call to the table. But she took my plate to a little room off to the side. I had to sit in this dingy corner with just room enough for one person. Every now and then they'd holler back there and ask me, "Have you got enough?"

I remember being so irked, I just wanted to get up and walk off. Because of my dad, I didn't. But from that point forward, even though she paid nicely, I would never do any work for her alone. I would only go with my dad if I had to. I never told my dad what happened.

For a while I turned sour against some of the things I had been taught in school. Things like the preamble of the Constitution, or the Constitution itself. When I was little, my ambition was to be an attorney. I wanted to learn about the Constitution. I was taught it was one of the greatest things. Then I found out that when the Constitution was written, the black man was not considered a whole person. So this could not have been written with us in mind. I couldn't believe that on the one hand they're saying this is the greatest country in the world with all this freedom, and I can't even go to the movies here if I want to.

One of the things in school every morning was to say the preamble and to salute the flag. I got to the point where I got poisoned against that. I didn't care anything for the preamble. I didn't care about singing "America the Beautiful" because it wasn't beautiful to me. I had gotten to the point in elementary school that I wouldn't even hold my hand over my heart.

The movement made a difference because it made me realize that somebody else agreed that this was not right. And it wasn't just one other person. There were thousands of people who felt the same way, who felt we've got to turn this nation around. This is wrong.

One of my major excitements was going to a mass meeting and finding whites there, and from different geographic corners of the country. You'd sit on your porch over here and be told by one group of whites, "You're black, get back, this is not for you." And then over there there's another group of whites saying, "We're all equal, but you've got to fight for it. And you got to fight for it by getting out there and being counted in numbers."

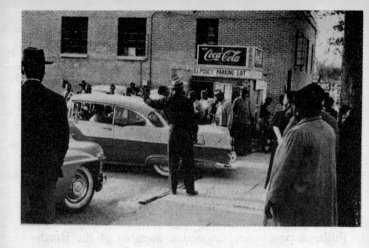

Waiting for a car pool during the bus boycott in Montgomery, Alabama.

2. The Montgomery Bus Boycott and the Beginning of the Movement

The modern civil rights movement is often said to have started with the Montgomery Bus Boycott of 1955–56. For over a year, nearly fifty thousand blacks in Montgomery stayed off the buses. They walked, hitchhiked, carpooled, all in protest against the discriminatory and demeaning system of segregation.

In Montgomery, black riders were about seventy-five percent of all bus passengers. Still they had to give their seats to any standing white person, or stand themselves over empty seats in the "white only" area.

Jo Ann Robinson was a teacher at Alabama State College and head of the Women's Political Council, a group of black professional women. E. D. Nixon was past president of the Montgomery NAACP, a Pullman porter, and an active member of the Brotherhood of Sleeping Car Porters. Both had urged a bus boycott for many years. They waited only for the right moment.

On December 1, 1955, a forty-three-year-old seamstress named Rosa Parks, who had worked as secretary at the local NAACP, was arrested and charged with violating the segregation laws for refusing to get up and give her bus seat to a white person. The night Rosa Parks was arrested, Robinson and some friends printed thousands of leaflets calling for a one-day boycott. The leaflet read:

Another Negro woman has been arrested and thrown in jail because she refused to get up out of her seat on the bus for a white person to sit down. It is the second time since the Claudette Colvin case that a Negro woman has been arrested for the same thing. This has to be stopped. Negroes have rights too, for if Negroes did not ride the buses, they could not operate. Three-fourths of the riders are Negroes, yet we are arrested, or have to stand over empty seats. If we do not do something to stop these arrests, they will continue. The next time it may be you, or your daughter, or mother. This woman's case will come up on Monday. We are, therefore, asking every Negro to stay off the buses Monday in protest of the arrest and trial. Don't ride the buses to work, to town, to school, or anywhere on Monday. You can afford to stay out of school for one day if you have no other way to go except by bus. You can also afford to stay out of town for one day. If you work, take a cab, or walk. But please, children and grown-ups, don't ride the bus at all on Monday. Please stay off of all buses Monday.

Monday morning the buses rolled through the black neighborhoods empty. The boycott was virtually total. Fueled by the success of the one-day action, thousands at a church meeting that night voted to continue the boycott. The Montgomery Improvement Association (MIA) was organized to coordinate boycott activities. Dr. Martin Luther King, Jr., the new young pastor of the Dexter Avenue Baptist Church, had recently moved to Montgomery from Atlanta, Georgia. An eloquent speaker who was willing to assume additional responsibilities, he was elected president of the MIA. The Montgomery Bus Boycott thus began not only the civil rights movement, but also Dr. King's remarkable career as a world-famous leader of that movement.

Some Montgomery segregationists were violent in their response to the bus boycott. Reverend Ralph Abernathy was a boycott leader with Dr. King. His home and church were bombed. Dr. King's home was also bombed, and so was that of community leader E. D. Nixon. Even with these attacks, the success of the boycott inspired similar protests in other southern cities and towns. Black ministers throughout the South whose churches had supported the boycott established a new group that became the Southern Christian Leadership Conference (SCLC) with Reverend Martin Luther King, Jr., as president. SCLC, with other civil rights groups, was a main organizer of protest activities in the 1960s.

Rosa Parks has been recognized as a hero of the movement for her determined resistance to discrimination that began the Montgomery Bus Boycott. But a careful reading of that first boycott leaflet shows that before Rosa Parks there was Claudette Colvin.

CLAUDETTE COLVIN

Claudette Colvin was fifteen years old in 1955. On her own she defied the segregation laws on the Montgomery city buses when she refused to give up her seat to a white person. She was arrested, found guilty, and fined. Nine months after Claudette's arrest, the boycott began. Claudette Colvin was ahead of her time.

When I grew up, the South was segregated. Very much so. Your parents had taught you that you had a place. You knew that much. In the city you had the signs. You have to stay here, you have to drink out of this fountain, you can't eat at this counter. I thought segregation was horrible. My first anger I remember was when I wanted to go to the rodeo. Daddy bought my sister boots and bought us both cowboy hats.

That's as much of the rodeo as we got. The show was at the coliseum, and it was only for white kids. I was nine or ten.

It bothered me when I got old enough to understand. You could buy dry goods at the five-and-ten-cent stores, Kress's, H. L. Green, J. J. Newberry's. You could buy, but you couldn't sit down and eat there. When I realized that, I was really angry.

Certain stores you couldn't try on the clothes. You could just ask for what you wanted. I remember this girl in school. She was mulatto. We used to get her to go in Nachman's to try on hats for us. Because she was white-looking, they didn't know. We had one friend whose father had money. So if she saw a hat or shoes at Nachman's, she used to push this girl to go in and get it. We knew this girl could pass, and we just wanted to be able to say that somebody with black blood has been in there to try on a hat or a pair of shoes. This was before the boycott.

At that time we were rebelling in different ways. I was always rebellious, but my mother said this is the way it is. The white people—they own everything, they bought everything, they built it—you know the whole story. That made me angry.

I talked about it with my friends. We would say the older people let white people get away with it. They never said they didn't like it. Older black people were always respectful to the white people. But the younger blacks began to rebel.

In school we were always taught that we had to study hard. We had to learn and think twice as hard as a white person in order to get ahead. You must be educated. I went to Booker T. Washington. When I was in the ninth grade, my history teacher was always discussing current events.

Most of the schoolteachers at Booker T. Washington came from Dexter Avenue Baptist Church, where Dr. Martin Luther King was pastor. And most of them got their education in the North. I think they were just pricking our minds to see how we were thinking.

My mind got pricked. This history teacher was tall and real dark. She'd say, "I'm a real African. I'm a pure-blooded African." We really didn't know what she was talking about. She was the blackest teacher in the school. In those days we would size up people by the color of their skin.

"How could she stand up there saying these things?" we used to say. She kept pricking our minds. "Do you feel good about yourself, you feel good inside? What do you hate about yourselves? Are you studying hard?" And she'd say, "You won't let anything bother you and stop you, regardless of your complexion." She tried to get that in our minds. She said there's no such thing as good hair. We were worried about good hair.

We had to write essays about how we felt about ourselves. And in those days when a teacher told you to do something, you had to do it, whether you wrote one line or more.

I wrote I was an American. My essay was that I felt clean, and I didn't see why we couldn't try on clothes in the store. I said I wasn't going to wear a cap before I tried on a hat. In those days you had to wear a cap or a head scarf to try on a hat so that "grease" wouldn't get on the hat. And I said furthermore, why do we have to press our hair and have to straighten our hair to look good?

The teacher read my essay before the class. Everybody said, "Oh, Claudette! You're crazy. You'll never get a boyfriend." And my closest friends said, "Claudette, would you really come to school with your hair kinky?" Well, the teacher really had pricked my mind, so I went home and I washed my hair and I didn't straighten it. My sister and my mother said I was crazy. When I came into school, everybody said I was crazy. I looked like a six- or seven-year-old. I had my hair in little braids all over. When you're thirteen, you don't wear your hair in all those braids. Maybe two.

My other sister had died not too long before, and they all said I was upset because she had passed. I said no. It was the essay I wrote. They all had said I wouldn't have the nerve to do that to my hair, and that I was just joking. Or that I was trying to get a good grade. But I wasn't joking. I actually did it. And I did lose my boyfriend. Teenagers figure you must be crazy if you'd lose your boyfriend. But that was okay. He said, "Claudette, I didn't believe that you would come to school this way."

I kept wearing it like that, and they kept me out of school plays. Everybody at school had heard about my braids. I wore them until I proved to them that I wasn't crazy. I had to convince them that I wasn't crazy.

Claudette became aware of civil rights as a public issue with the arrest of Jeremiah Reeves.

At my school the reason we got into it was because a boy named Jeremiah Reeves was arrested for supposedly raping a white woman, which he did not do. The authorities kept him in jail until he came of age,

and then they electrocuted him. He was from Booker
T. Washington, my school. He was the drummer for
the school band. His father was a delivery man at the
same store that Rosa Parks worked at. I was in the
ninth grade when it happened. And that anger is still
in me from seeing him being held as a minor until he
came of age.

That was the first time I heard talk about the
NAACP. I thought it was just a small organization. I
didn't know it was nationwide. I heard about it
through the teachers. Some people said that the reason
they convicted Jeremiah was to prove to the NAACP
that they couldn't take over the South. Our school
would take up collections for the NAACP, and we'd
have movies for Jeremiah to try and help pay for good
lawyers for him. Our rebellion and anger came with
Jeremiah Reeves.

At that time, teenagers didn't like to ride the special
school bus too much. If you had to stay after school
for band practice or a rehearsal, or hang around for
after-school activities, and you missed the special, you
still could ride on your school pass, but on the regular
bus.

On the regular buses there were signs on the side
saying "Colored" with an arrow this way and
"White" with an arrow this way. The motorman
could adjust the signs. He could direct people to sit
where he wanted them to.

You knew that you weren't supposed to sit opposite
a white person, or in front of a white person. The
number of seats varied in different communities. Depending on whether there was a larger black population, there could be the first two or four rows reserved
for white people.

On March 2, 1955, I got on the bus in front of Dexter Avenue Church. I went to the middle. No white people were on the bus at that time. It was mostly schoolchildren. I wasn't thinking about anything in particular. I think I had just finished eating a candy bar. Then the bus began to fill up. White people got on and began to stare at me. The bus motorman asked me to get up. We were getting into the square where all the buses take their routes in either direction. A colored lady got on, and she was pregnant. I was sitting next to the window. The seat next to me was the only seat unoccupied. She didn't realize what was going on. She didn't know that the bus driver had asked me to get up. She just saw the empty seat and sat next to me. A white lady was sitting across the aisle from me, and it was against the law for you to sit in the same aisle with a white person.

The bus driver looked back through the rearview mirror and again told me to get up. I didn't. I knew he was talking to me. He said, "Hey, get up!" I didn't say anything. When I didn't get up, he didn't move the bus. He said before he'd drive on, I'd have to get up. People were saying, "Why don't you get up? Why don't you get up?" One girl said, "She knows she has to get up." Then another girl said, "She doesn't have to. Only one thing you have to do is stay black and die."

The white people were complaining. The driver stopped the bus and said, "This can't go on." Then he got up and said, "I'm going to call the cops." First a traffic patrolman came on the bus and he asked, "Are any of you gentleman enough to get up and give this pregnant lady your seat?" There were two black men in the back of the bus who were sanitation workers. They got up, and the pregnant lady went and sat in the back. That left me still sitting by the window.

I remained there, and the traffic patrolman said, "Aren't you going to get up?"

I said, "No. I do not have to get up. I paid my fare, so I do not have to get up. It's my constitutional right to sit here just as much as that lady. It's my constitutional right!" The words just came into my mind. That history teacher and my literature teacher, they were just pricking our minds. In literature, she was an unorthodox teacher. She didn't teach us regular literature. She said, "If you can read and write, you can read it yourself." She taught us the Constitution, the Bill of Rights, the Articles of Confederation. She talked about the Magna Carta and the history of old England. "Give me liberty, or give me death," Patrick Henry's speech.

Anyway, the traffic patrolman told the bus driver that he had no jurisdiction, and that he would have to call the regular policemen. When they got on the bus, I was speaking so fast I don't think they realized I was a southerner. I don't think they realized I knew what I was doing. The busman just kept saying, "She won't get up, she won't get up." He was turning red.

I kept saying, "He has no right . . . this is my constitutional right . . . you have no right to do this!" I just kept talking and I never stopped. My mother used to say, "She can out-talk forty lawyers." And I just kept blabbing things out and I never stopped. That was worse than stealing, you know, talking back to a white person. I had this high-pitched voice, too.

The police knocked my books down. One took one wrist, the other grabbed the other, and they were pulling me off the bus, just like you see on the TV now. I was really struggling. They put me in the car. Somebody must have said they didn't have handcuffs on me and I might run away, so they put handcuffs on me. And then they took me to City Hall. I remember one of the men saying, "What happened to this black bitch? This is a black whore." He said, "Take her to Atmore [state prison] and get rid of her."

The bus motorman didn't tell them I was a regular student. So I think they thought I was a passionate person who didn't know southern ways. I think that's what saved me, that and my squeaky high-pitched tone of voice.

Other kids got home and told Mama what happened. She already knew how hurt I was about Jeremiah Reeves. She knew this wasn't a one-day thing. This was a rebellious time that started with Jeremiah.

I didn't know what was happening. I was just angry. Like a teenager might be. I was just downright angry. You know, it felt like I was helpless. And I just couldn't get over Jeremiah being framed.

Mama knew Fred Gray, the attorney. And Mama let him and E. D. Nixon handle it. Fred Gray told me to participate in a group that was run by Rosa Parks. This was before she was arrested, before the boycott. Someone in the family said, "Rosa Parks? She's from Pine Level." She and my mother were playmates together.

When I first met her, she talked about my mother. Then she said that I wasn't what she expected. "I was looking for someone tough and fiery-looking," she said. And I didn't look like that. I was tall and skinny and I wasn't fiery-looking. I wore little round glasses. Then she talked about her organization. There were more kids, she said, who would be interested to hear my story, who were angry like me. They were kids from the other side of town and most of them went to Carver High School. They always thought better kids went to Carver than to Booker T. Washington. In the group most of the kids I talked to were middle-class children. I didn't stay involved too long, because it was the other side of town.

If I'd have been living in Rosa's community, it would have been more uplifting, because you would have had someone to talk to, and someone to walk to and from school with. But in my community I did not have that kind of support. In my community they were mostly working-class people. They weren't into politics. They were just hardworking people.

In Booker T. Washington, I was in the eleventh grade, and kids were mostly into dating and things like that. They weren't into any heavy intellectual things. The kids in school wanted to avoid me because they said, "She's the girl that was in the bus thing." Sometimes I felt I did something wrong because I lost a lot of friends. And you know how it is when you're a teenager.

We had a saying that black people would be free in a hundred years. You know, from 1863 to 1963. But no one wanted to do anything about it individually, or get together and say, "No more. I'm hurting, and I don't like this." The funny thing was they all wanted change, but they didn't know how to go about it.

I heard about Rosa Parks's arrest through a college friend, and that there was going to be a boycott because they arrested Rosa Parks. I was glad. I met Jo Ann Robinson during the boycott. She was writing letters to the white newspapers. We shook hands and she said she'd heard of me, and that my schoolteacher had told her about what a spunky student I was.

I didn't feel bad that all the talk was about Rosa Parks. Things keep going around in circles. There is

always a need for a demonstration here or there. And
once they told me she was my mother's friend, she
was like a family member. It didn't bother me. If she
had been a total stranger, it probably would have hurt
me a little bit. We had the same ideas, the same
thoughts.

My sister Mary once mentioned something about
Rosa Parks. She said, "They never mention you. One
day someone might mention you. They'll go through
the court files and want to know who was Claudette
Colvin."

I'm not sorry I did it. I'm glad I did it. The revo-
lution was there and the direction it was going in. My
generation was angry. And people just wanted a
change. They just wanted a change.

JOSEPH LACEY

*Many schoolchildren participated in the boycott.
Joe Lacey was thirteen years old when the boycott began. He walked to school every day of the
boycott.*

Jo Ann Robinson worked over at Alabama State [at
that time an all-black college]. She was a great person.
She helped write and distribute the first leaflets. Some
of the leaflets fell into the wrong hands. The whites'
hands. They notified the powers-that-be of the anticipated boycott. It was supposed to have been a sur-
prise thing, but then there was lots of news coverage.
The word spread around town like I don't know what.
I recall my grandmother saying that some of her
friends were threatened by their bosses not to partic-

ipate and told if they did, they would lose their jobs.

When the boycott started, I just couldn't wait for morning to come because I wanted to see what was happening. I walked to school. As the buses passed me and my schoolmates, we said, "Nobody's on the bus! Nobody's on the bus!" It was just a beautiful thing. It was a day to behold to see nobody on the bus.

Everybody stuck together on the boycott. It lasted over a year, and we walked and enjoyed walking. Everybody felt like a part of the struggle because everybody had a part. Even some whites stayed off in sympathy, I'm sure. Black drivers would pass you along the street, and if they were going your way, they'd stop and pick you up. Most persons going across town would go through this area right below the school, and you could stand on the corner and holler, "Going across?" and that's all they'd need to hear. "Come on, get in the car," and they'd take you across town.

A lot of persons were arrested because they were picking up people. Many were arrested for all kinds of trumped-up charges, but still they picked people up.

There was a central car pickup downtown at Posey's parking lot. Also at certain corners, certain churches, certain locations, you knew that a station wagon would come by, and you'd get a ride. Dean's drugstore was another pickup spot.

The churches had station wagons. The Montgomery Improvement Association (MIA) bought them with contributions coming from the North. MIA couldn't be licensed to shuttle people. So to get around state law, most churches had a station wagon with their names, not MIA, on it.

* * *

I vividly remember the court decision on bus integration. I remember the celebration at the mass meetings. And I remember seeing it on the Douglas Edward news, and feeling that we had won. It was a blessing. It was just a thrilling thing.

I can remember the first time getting on a bus after the decision. I remember thinking I didn't have to go to the back. Before the boycott, every time we'd go for church picnics, we'd rent a city bus and I'd go sit right behind the driver. You see, that was the only time I could sit behind the driver, when the buses were chartered for that purpose. After the boycott, I'd sit right behind the driver. It gave me pleasure.

FRED TAYLOR

Fred Taylor grew up in Montgomery and was thirteen years old when the bus boycott began.

I remember folks talking about what had happened to Mrs. Parks. Reverend Abernathy talked about it, and I remember the church raising money for the boycott. I had to slip to go to the mass meetings up at my church because my grandmother didn't want me to go. I remember how fearful she was for me. I had to lie about where I had been. I thought my grandmama was mean. She said, "Boy, you just can't go." And I said, "Why?"

As a kid I never was afraid. And I was puzzled as to why my grandparents were so afraid of what was going on. Now, looking back, I understand—because of the intimidation and fear for losing their lives and all of that. My grandmother was a domestic worker.

She was a maid for white folks. And my grandfather was a porter for a furniture company, delivering furniture in the city of Montgomery. My grandmother went along with the boycott and did not get on the bus. Although she was afraid, that was the thing to do. Her employer came by and picked her up. That's how she got to work.

At the time the boycott began, all these news reporters started following my pastor and Dr. King around. Something I guess happened to me, particularly as I began to listen to Dr. King's speeches. I can remember going to mass meetings during the boycott and hearing him speak. You know the mastery of the English language that Dr. King had. I can remember the euphoria, and how he would turn people on.

He would talk about the fact that you are somebody and you are important. This was compared to my orientation of being put down or told, "Boy, you're not going to be anything." A classic example was people would say, "You knotty-head boy, why don't you sit down?"

But when Dr. King started talking, he'd say, "You are somebody." And that began to rub off on me. It was right during the boycott that I began to have a different assessment of myself as an individual and to feel my sense of worth. Not only did it affect me, but I began to look at my family and how the white community related to them.

The boycotters challenged the segregation laws in court. Finally in November 1956 the United States Supreme Court declared the bus segregation laws unconstitutional. On December 21,

*nearly thirteen months after the protest had be-
gun, blacks again rode the Montgomery City
Lines buses.*

Before the boycott I'd taken the buses and gone to
the back. After the boycott was over, I participated
with a group of students riding predominantly white
routes, deliberately sitting in the front of the bus. In
our orientation for this particular project we were told
to make sure we were well groomed. I sat up there
very proudly. I would sit beside a white man, but I
consciously did not sit by a white woman. I can remember a boy, Jeremiah Reeves, who got electrocuted
for allegedly raping a white woman.

In some instances when I would sit by a white man,
he would jump up and leave. I was thinking, "Ain't
nothing wrong with me. I don't stink, I took a bath
this morning." When they'd jump up, I just thought
it was sort of strange.

PRINCELLA HOWARD

*Princella Howard was eight years old when the
boycott started. She and her six-year-old sister,
Barbara, grew up in a family that was actively
involved in MIA activities. Both girls participated in the boycott and went on to become student leaders in the Montgomery civil rights
movement of the 1960s.*

What's so amazing is that it only takes a few. You
see, it was just a handful of people before the bus
boycott. Nobody in their wildest imagination could
have conceived that that kind of organization and co-

operation would have been forthcoming. We were just
a group of people going about daily life getting ready
for Christmas. That was the biggest thing on
all the kids' minds. Santa Claus. And then overnight
it changed from just a sleepy little town.

One thing we all knew: something had to give. I'm
sure everybody understood that. Blacks and whites. It
was like a keg full of dynamite. Even in the quietness,
it was too quiet. The whole country was too quiet.

The boycott was a real movement. It was so powerful. In a year you can build a great momentum. It
brought together even people who were generally at
odds with each other. We were very well aware at the
time that Dexter Avenue [Martin Luther King's
church] was a church for rich black people. It wasn't
for just everybody. It was remarkable to see the rich
blacks and the poor ones at mass meetings interested
in the same thing. I was eight and nine years old, but
I understood clearly. Kids know when some people
look down at you. They know it very well. Those
were some of the victories that are seldom mentioned—the victories within our race that were also
taking place.

GWENDOLYN PATTON

*Gwen Patton moved from Detroit to Montgomery
after the boycott had ended.*

In the summer of 1960, it was decided by all the family members after my mother passed that I should
[leave Detroit and] come home to Montgomery. When
I came to live here, I'd get on the bus with my grandmother. She would always go to the back and I would

always plop right up front. You know, we had won a victory and all. One day there were no people on the bus and I went to the back with my grandmother. I called her "Mommy." I said, "Mommy, why do you sit in the back? You worked so hard, and you all walked."

She said, "Darling, the bus boycott was not about sitting next to white people. It was about sitting anywhere you please."

The Little Rock Nine, with officers of the NAACP.

3. Different Classrooms: Segregation and Integration in the Schools

In 1954, in a case called *Brown v. Board of Education of Topeka*, the United States Supreme Court ruled that separating the races in schools deprives Negro children of equal educational opportunities. "Separate educational facilities are inherently unequal," Chief

Justice Warren wrote. In addition, he said, school segregation creates in minority children "a feeling of inferiority as to their status in the community that may
affect their hearts and minds in a way unlikely ever
to be undone." The Court declared school segregation
laws unconstitutional.

The decision stunned and enraged southern segregationists. In March 1956 a group of U.S. Senators
and Representatives from the eleven states of the Old
Confederacy signed a statement called the "Southern
Manifesto." In it, they declared their opposition to the
Supreme Court decision and urged that schools fight
any attempts to integrate. As a result of resistance by
segregationists, which was sometimes violent, most
southern schools were not integrated until ten to
twenty years after the Supreme Court decision in the
Brown case.

Black children's experiences in segregated schools
differed widely. In some classrooms, teachers were
hesitant to talk about civil rights for fear of antagonizing the white establishment. In others, teachers instilled in their students a pride in black achievement.
As in all schools, segregated or integrated, some
teachers repeated past lessons so that few were inspired and most were bored. Others challenged their
students to think, to stretch. As Claudette Colvin said
of her teachers, they were "pricking our minds." The
young people who tell their stories in the section on
segregated schools reflect the full range of this experience.

In every black school, the students knew that their
facilities and materials were inferior to those in white
schools. "You really felt the second-class citizenship
in the educational system," says James Roberson,
himself a former school principal. "Never receiving

a new textbook was quite revealing to me. Our books were from white schools, and used. You always got books with marks in them.''

But despite the limited resources, black children in segregated schools were at least in a safe environment. Their first experiences of integration were startling by contrast. Although none of them anticipated warm welcomes, neither did they expect the depth and extent of the hostility they encountered from white students and often teachers. Yet they persisted, and in that persistence exhibited an extraordinary strength and single-mindedness of purpose.

Myrna Carter

Myrna Carter attended segregated elementary and high schools in Birmingham in the 1950s.

We heard about the *Brown* decision, but with our schools being segregated, many teachers were very afraid to really discuss things. We did have some who were outspoken and willing to talk with you and let you know exactly what was going on. I will never forget Mrs. Maggie Hrowbuski in elementary school. One day when the World Series was about to start, she asked the class, ''Who are you pulling for?''

And the whole class said, ''The Dodgers! The Dodgers!''

She asked, ''Do you know why?'' Everybody went blank. It was probably something you heard your parents say. Then she gave us a lecture on Jackie Robinson. I will never forget that. She was a very dedicated person, and she believed in teaching us about our own people. When she got through lecturing us on Jackie Robinson and how the Dodgers were the first team to allow a black to become a member, well, then we knew why we were rooting for the Dodgers.

LARRY RUSSELL

Larry Russell was a student in Birmingham during the 1950s and 1960s. He attended segregated schools.

We had Negro Education Week in school, where your teachers would assign you a task of finding something that was done by a "colored" person. That was the term used then. Black kids had very limited knowledge of blacks' contribution to this society. The teacher would list famous people, and always heading the group would be George Washington Carver. You can imagine that if there were only ten or fifteen names on the list, and there are maybe thirty to thirty-five students, George Washington Carver and the peanut goes around many times. Everybody is sitting there bored, and the next year you come back and it's right back to George Washington Carver and the peanut again. I can remember from the time I can remember being in school, we dwelt on the peanut.

ROY DEBERRY

Roy DeBerry went to an all-black school in Holly Springs, Mississippi.

We went to a rural school. There was one teacher, Henry Boyd, who taught first through eighth grades, all in one room. He was black. We had to walk about three miles to school. When we got there, we had to do chores. We had one big potbelly stove that was in the middle of the room, and we had to get the wood for the stove. Because we didn't have a water supply, we had to go to a spring, which was about a mile away, to pick the water up and bring it back. We got fresh springwater every day.

There was not even an outhouse for the boys. Just the woods. I think there was an outhouse for the girls. And of course there was no electricity, so if it was stormy or dark outside we had to use an oil lamp. We also had to clean up in the afternoon because there was no such thing as a janitor.

Mr. Boyd was a history teacher. He talked to us about Booker T. Washington and W. E. B. Du Bois. He talked to us about blacks who had been involved in early struggles. It made us proud. He was kind of an orator and a very colorful character. He had a way of making history come alive.

FRED TAYLOR

Fred Taylor was a student in Montgomery, Alabama, during the bus boycott.

I was in a segregated school—Booker T. Washington High School. I remember how we as students wanted to talk about what was going on in Montgomery. And how the teachers were in some instances discouraging us from bringing up the discussion. As I think about it in retrospect, they were nervous about losing their jobs. I mean, in Montgomery at the time the only professional jobs you had were teacher or preacher.

You could count the number of black lawyers or doctors in the city.

I remember an incident while I was in high school. I had an opportunity to participate in an oratorical contest sponsored by the Montgomery Improvement Association, which was the movement organization at the time. I had as my coach my high school English teacher. She was a brilliant woman. She knew Shakespeare and all of that. But I was familiar with what would win in the oratorical contest. It was a contest on the movement. She wanted me to write a speech which was mild, nonconfrontational, with non-movement language in it. Just a nice high school piece. I knew that that wouldn't make it. What I did was I wrote a speech which I knew would be in the running. When I was with her, I practiced her speech. When I got by myself, I practiced my speech.

On the night of the contest when I got up there, I forgot both speeches, and I broke down and started crying. I just cried and cried, and walked off the stage. It was a real tension for me. I had love and respect for my teacher, but at the same time there was something on the inside of me which was driving me.

SCHOOL INTEGRATION

The following stories are about those black students who were the first to integrate all-white schools. With every attempt at integration, there was resistance from segregationists. For Ricky and Pat Shuttlesworth, the violence was so great they never even entered the school they were trying to integrate. For the others who were able to enroll, there were taunts, even attacks, by other students, and often shameful behavior by teachers.

As Ernest Green from Little Rock, Arkansas, says, "You'd be crazy not to have fear." But these young people also had a sense of perspective and even humor about what was happening. Their courage made a difference not only in each of their individual lives, but for all the others who have followed.

In the fall of 1957 in Birmingham, less than a year after their church parsonage had been bombed, Reverend and Mrs. Shuttlesworth tried to enroll their two oldest daughters, Pat and Ricky, in the largest all-white high school in the city. Their son, Fred, was in elementary school at the time.

RICKY SHUTTLESWORTH

In 1957 I was starting the ninth grade and supposed to go to Parker, an all-black high school. Phillips was all-white. Where I lived, you'd have to go past Phillips to get to Parker. It didn't make sense. Phillips had much more to offer. At Parker we didn't have the equipment or the facilities. I knew Phillips was a better school. So we decided to enroll. It was an effort to break down segregation. Daddy said, "You're going," and I trusted his judgment.

I never really showed fear because I was always taught to be strong. Being a "PK," a preacher's kid, you couldn't always let your feelings show. A lot of times I had played out a scenario in my mind. But it was so frightening that sometimes you didn't deal with it. You just did it. I'm sure I was nervous the day we went, but then again I was with my father and that alleviated some of the nervousness.

I didn't expect the mob that was there. It's not that I expected a positive reception either. They hadn't been positive for the other things we did, like the bus rides or the sit-ins. But even before we pulled up, when we turned up the street, we saw this tremendous number of people. All whites. Everywhere. I don't remember any of the dialogue that went on. I just thought, Are we going in there?

I could not believe that Daddy got out of the car. The crowd started to beat him. Mother got out. Then I started to get out of the car to get to my mother and my father, and somebody slammed the door on my right ankle. There was mass confusion, but I have blanked it out of my mind. My sister and I have never talked about what happened that day.

Somehow we were all back in the car. Reverend Phifer was with us that day. I remember Daddy saying, "Don't run the stop sign." We went to a hospital. Daddy was on the stretcher, and he wanted to know if everybody was okay. We sat in the hall for a while, waiting. I didn't know what was happening, if Daddy was okay. He was broken down, shallow breathing, and I thought he was dying. I couldn't believe that people would hurt him like that. They beat him with chains and stuff. I was just in shock that they were so vicious.

Somebody said we did it in the name of freedom. What my sister said sticks in my mind. If she had to go back in that crowd again, she said she would have a fork as a weapon. But we were nonviolent, and as I think about it, what good would a fork do?

We discovered at the hospital that my mother had been stabbed. That was even more upsetting. She was stabbed in the hip, and I wasn't aware of it. She never let us know how she was hurt or how she was suffering.

PAT SHUTTLESWORTH

We were told we were going to integrate Phillips. With Daddy being the leader, he wanted his first two kids to be involved. I'm not as patient and nonviolent as Ricky and Daddy are. If anybody hit me, I was ready to hit back. But I had been told you can't do anything but walk in the school. They prepared us.

The car pulled up, and there were mobs of people saying, "Niggers go home!" and shouting obscenities. All these vicious-looking people saying things you hadn't heard before out loud. It didn't make sense to me to get out of the car with all those people surrounding us. But Daddy was going to try to do it anyway.

They started to attack him. Then my mother got out because he was being attacked, and that's when she got stabbed in the hip. She was trying to tell us to stay in the car, but we didn't want to hear. We were going to go out to help our father. There was just so much confusion. Even though he had been beaten, Daddy had enough strength to work his way around and get back in the car. We sped off. Ricky got her foot slammed in the door. I never got out at all. At the hospital when we saw there was blood, we knew my mother had been stabbed. The hardest part was when my father was on that stretcher in the hospital, and he was telling us to be brave and that you have to forgive people.

I don't look at it now when it's on TV because it's

painful. I can't watch it. I get angry all over again. I don't like crowds to this day.

FRED SHUTTLESWORTH, JR.

It was just another day at school for me until I got back. When I got home, they were all there. My father was in bed with all these people around him. I guess it was the first time white folks had been in our house. News reporters and so forth.

On TV there was this man getting beat up with chains, not just ropes. It was happening right next to our car. I said, "Who is this?" and my father said, "That's me. It's all right, Junior."

It was shocking. I mean, at the same time I saw Daddy in the bed, I saw him beaten on TV.

The Phillips High School incident had a powerful impact on other young black people in Birmingham. The following comments are typical:

JAMES ROBERSON

I felt tremendous anger at these people who had hurt them. The thought that nothing was going to be done about it was just devastating to me. There is something wrong when you actually stab a lady for no apparent reason other than the fact that she wanted to go into a school.

I felt a rage. I wished I could just go out and get a gun and kill them all because they really didn't deserve to live. I thought, If I was God, I would just wave my hand and say, "Away with all the white people who hated black people."

MYRNA CARTER

The time Reverend Shuttlesworth tried to enroll his daughters in Phillips High School was the most frightening day. I believe it was the worst day that I can remember. We actually saw hundreds and hundreds of white people standing around watching others beat a black man with chains just because he wanted to enroll his children. And no one was going to his defense. They felt justified in what they were doing. To actually witness something as brutal as that went real, real deep with me.

THE LITTLE ROCK NINE

Although the Supreme Court had ruled in the *Brown* school case that segregation in public schools was unconstitutional, many communities ignored the ruling. Supporters of integration then had to go to court to sue individual school systems that were segregated. In Arkansas, as in other southern communities, the NAACP, which had originally brought the *Brown* case, began to plan for school integration. Daisy Bates, who with her husband published the black newspaper the *Arkansas State Press* in Little Rock, was the president of the Arkansas NAACP.

Little Rock appeared to be a progressive southern city. The school board had worked out a desegregation plan, and nine black children were selected to attend Central High School beginning September 3, 1957, three years after the Supreme Court integration decision. But Arkansas governor Orval Faubus moved to block the integration plans. He called out the Arkansas National Guard. Troops surrounded the school, admitting only white students and blocking the black students at bayonet point.

Eight of the black students had met at Daisy Bates's house and gone from there to the school as a group. Elizabeth Eckford, the ninth, hadn't gotten the message to meet at Mrs. Bates's house. She went to Central High School alone and was surrounded by a raging mob of whites screaming racial epithets. Some yelled, "Lynch her! Lynch her!" Elizabeth described one moment: "I looked into the face of an old woman and it seemed a kind face, but when I looked at her again, she spat on me."

Young black people throughout the country watched the events unfolding in Little Rock. In Detroit, Gwen Patton watched the Little Rock riots on television:

> They were brave kids. Brave kids. In fact when I came to live in Alabama, I realized I wasn't as brave as they were. Somebody suggested I go to the University of Alabama, but I claimed I didn't want to go to a white school. I liked being black, I liked being Negro, I wanted to go to Tuskegee. I'd read about Booker T. Washington and George Washington Carver, and I wouldn't dare miss an opportunity to go to the school that they started and pulled together. But I also think that was a cover for fear of what I would have to undergo. I knew the kind of personality I had. I would not be able to withstand that kind of abuse.

Mary Gadson was in Birmingham, Alabama, at the time.

We were so worried about the Little Rock Nine. Our hearts were always out for them when the news would come on, because we were afraid they would get hurt or killed. They had to have something in them to make them do that. It took more than courage. It was almost as if that was their purpose for being born. In my mind they were a remarkable set of people.

ERNEST GREEN

Ernest Green was one of the Little Rock Nine. He was the only senior in the group.

In the spring of 1957, the Little Rock school board finally agreed to desegregate grades ten through twelve. It was going to occur at Central High School [an all-white school].

We all knew Central. And in many cases the course books that we used were hand-me-downs from Central. You could tell because they had Central students' names in them. You didn't have to be a rocket scientist to figure out that the building, the course curriculum, the laboratory facilities, all of that was significantly different from what we had at Horace Mann, the black high school.

In Little Rock you never thought of yourself as being "Deep South." Deep South was going to Jackson, Mississippi, or Birmingham, Alabama. The year before we went to Central, both the city buses in Little Rock and the public libraries were integrated without any problems. The university had accepted some black students, and while it was difficult, they were surviving and doing their course work. So my expectations were that there would be words and taunts, but over a period of time that would blow over. I didn't think there'd be anything I couldn't handle.

And it seemed to me an opportunity to participate in something new. I knew it was going to be a change in Little Rock—I was smart enough to figure that out—but I didn't realize it was going to have impact beyond Little Rock.

In the spring of '57, before we left school for the summer, each teacher gathered names of interested students. I put my name in, and that's where I left it. I don't think anybody really focused a great deal on it. If I got in, fine. I talked with my mother about it. She said if I wanted to go and I was accepted, she would support me.

People like my mother and my grandfather, who was a postman and had attempted to vote in the Democratic primary, really are the backbone of the southern resistance. They didn't take a high public position, but in many ways expressed their indignation, their anger, and attempted to turn things around. My mother and my aunt were part of a lawsuit in the 1940s that filed for equal pay for black and white teachers.

We kids did it mainly because we didn't know any better. But our parents were willing to put their careers, their homes on the line. To me that says a lot.

Some time before school started, we learned there were limits on what black students were going to be allowed to do. You knew that you weren't going to play football, be in the band or the class play, go to the prom. I had been in the school band for five years, from seventh grade through eleventh. Tenor sax. But this was an important enough breakthrough that all of these other activities, well, you could give them up.

For the first three weeks of the school term, Governor Faubus ordered the Arkansas National Guard to surround Central High to keep the black students out. Finally, a federal court judge ordered Faubus to remove the troops. The students were quietly brought into the school through a side door, while a riotous mob attacked black and white newspaper reporters nearby.

I never expected it to be life-threatening, which it was initially. I didn't have any real sense of how dangerous it could have been until we got home. We were in this huge school. I didn't hear any of the mob outside. When we were whisked out of school back to our homes, we sat there and watched it on TV. This is real, I thought. This is no day at the beach.

The whole period has been cast in such a monochrome color that you don't get any of the tension and discussions going on in the black community. I'll never forget that afternoon. There were lots of black people who didn't think this was such a terrific idea. They saw it as disruptive, upsetting their personal lives. This neighbor of mine said, "You kids are crazy. The federal government is never going to support you. You're going to be out there by yourself and never get back into the school." Now that was a real fear because I wanted to graduate that year.

President Eisenhower sent in the troops that night. There is an air force base about ten or fifteen miles from Little Rock. They were flying in a thousand paratroopers and support equipment. Lots of planes, probably a hundred or better, because they sent them in with all of their support materiel and jeeps and helicopters. I slept through all of that. Some people go hyper at crises. I usually get calm before and then I get hyper after I realize what I have done. So that night I didn't hear anything.

The next day we were picked up by the army at our individual houses and taken to Mrs. Bates's house, which was our gathering spot. From there we got into a station wagon. It was a convoy. They had a jeep in front, a jeep behind, and armed soldiers in each of them. I think there were machine-gun mounts on the back of the jeeps.

There were nine of us, and a station wagon was not very big. You had the driver, an officer in charge, and then us. We were all kind of squooshed in, riding along making jokes about it. There was no traffic, and no people were in front of Central. They had blocked off the school at least a half a block away. Nobody could enter without appropriate passes. I guess in army terms, they really had secured the area.

A helicopter was hovering overhead. You could see the news cameras across the street. And as we got out of the station wagon, a cordon of soldiers surrounded us. They marched, and we kind of strolled along, walking up the steps. Central is big, really built more like a college campus. The school is a couple of blocks long. A series of steps lead up to the front, which is very imposing. It was real drama going from the station wagon to the front door of the school. It probably took us four or five minutes just to walk up to the front of the steps.

Most people didn't believe Eisenhower would ever use that much force to get us back in school. I thought that that was important, but I had no idea of the importance of it beyond my particular situation. Also, we had been out of school for three weeks, so all of us were getting a little itchy about getting further behind in our course work.

Every day the troops would bring us to the school. Initially we each had a paratrooper who would wait outside the classroom to escort us to the next class, so that we were never alone. All the troop personnel at the school were white, even though the army was integrated at that time. The black men were kept back at the air force base. I've run into both black and white men who were in that 101st Airborne Division assigned to Little Rock. Each of them that I met has said how proud he was to be assigned to that duty.

The officers had sidearms in the school. The first day or so they had rifles inside the school. When Governor Faubus said Arkansas was occupied, that was true.

The army regulars and the 101st Airborne Division were withdrawn by November. Only the federalized Arkansas National Guard remained.

The first month with the troops and all of the media attention had been the point of high euphoria. In fact, conditions in the school were fairly tranquil. You had this great show of force. And also the most avid of the segregationists were boycotting classes at that point. When the segregationists realized that we weren't leaving, they started coming back. And when they came back, all hell started breaking loose. From around Thanksgiving until about March or April, it really was like having to fight hand-to-hand combat. It was trench warfare.

As they withdrew the troops from inside the corridors, you were subjected to all kinds of taunts, someone attempting to trip you, pour ink on you, in some other way ruin your clothing, and at worst, someone physically attacking you. I never had ink thrown on me. I got hit with water guns. We got calls at all times of the night—people saying they were going to have acid in the water guns and they were going to squirt it in our faces.

The biggest problems were in the halls and in physical education. In both places you had large numbers of students. The most difficult place for me was phys. ed., and that class was a requirement. The instructors just didn't want us there, and they didn't hide it a lot. When we were playing soccer or another activity, they didn't make any effort to pair you with students who were supportive. You got the feeling they deliberately put you with the most hostile kids.

When we'd come back to the locker room to shower, the students would always steam up the room and snap wet towels at us. It was a daily ritual. You just dreaded having to go to phys. ed.

You'd be crazy not to have fear. You kept fear in the back of your mind at all times, a fear that somebody was going to come over and physically harm you, and that nobody would come to your rescue. But we had to be nonviolent. Our nonviolence was an act of logic. We were nine students out of a couple of thousand.

The girls got it the most. There were six girls, three boys: Minniejean Brown, Elizabeth Eckford, Thelma Mothershed, Melba Pattillo, Gloria Ray, Carlotta Walls, Ernest Green, Terrence Roberts, Jefferson Thomas. With a couple of the girls, people took their femininity as a weakness and attempted to take advantage of that. The segregationists, the Citizens Council, were trying to figure which one of us they could break.

Then they really took after Minnie. The incident with Minnie and the chili happened in the student line in the cafeteria. This was right before Christmas. We were all looking forward to the holidays because this was tough duty. We just wanted to get a break.

A small band of students had really raised the level of harassment with Minnie. I'll never forget this kid. He was like a small dog snapping at Minnie with a steady stream of verbal abuse. He had figured out how many ways he could say "nigger." This kid just touched Minnie's last nerve. He was in front of her on the cafeteria line. I was behind her and I could see it coming. Before I could say "Minnie, don't do it. Forget him . . . " she had taken her bowl of chili and dumped it on his head. The chili just rolled down his face.

The cafeteria help in Central was black. They all broke into applause. The school board used the incident to suspend Minnie [but not the ones who harassed her], and then finally to expel her. And so coming back from Christmas, we were eight students. It was southern justice. They did what you'd expect them to do. In school, some students passed out little cards: "One down, eight to go."

Initially there were some white kids who attempted to be friendly with us, but they were pressured. The roughest period was after we came back for the second semester and the troops were withdrawn. The more avid racists really turned up the heat on other whites. If any of them were seen talking to us, they would get phone calls. They were called "nigger lover."

I remember doing a couple of radio programs with white kids interested in presenting a different point of view. Right after they appeared on the show, they received a great deal of hate mail and calls and pressure. I appreciated them trying to step forward, but we didn't have any sustained social relationship with them.

After the Christmas break, there was a great deal of pressure by the school authorities and business community to "normalize" conditions inside the school. There were still troops outside the school, but not in the halls and corridors. Well, of course, as the troops were withdrawn, the hostility increased. While the school authorities always talked about "normalizing" conditions, that year they just were never going to be normal.

I decided after the segregationists started coming back that I was going to make it through that year. Short of being shot, I could outlast anything they could give. I think it was a combination of the family support at home and the relationship that grew between the nine of us.

We each had different strengths and helped each other. I was probably the most stoic. As Terrence said, I only had to do it for one year. But I also thought that victory really was within our grasp. I thought we were probably driving them crazier than they were driving us. This really was a war of nerves, endurance. If we kept all that in front of us, we could win. Our personalities tended to complement each other. We were nine different people, nine different approaches to solving problems. We were a good fit.

We also got a burst of energy from the black part of Little Rock, which really began to rally around us. They showed support in lots of different ways. One of the black sororities provided concert tickets for us. And the black leadership in Little Rock was with us. My minister and a number of others continually made public statements about how important and brave they thought we were. Everybody was saying very encouraging things. While you were in there fighting those battles daily by yourself, it helped that other people thought very positively about what you were doing.

Loads of letters came in. We heard from everywhere. The *New York Post* ran a series on us and described my interest in jazz. One fellow who was living in New York wrote me, and we carried on a correspondence for a number of years.

Over six hundred students were graduating, and there were honors and scholarships and all that. It's the irony of my class that no matter what any of the others did that night, they were all going to be overshadowed by one event—my graduation. I mean, they could be magna cum laude and have 59,000 scholarships, but that wasn't going to be the hook that people were going to remember.

We sat in these seats, and I had a space on both sides because nobody wanted to sit next to me. To get your diploma, you had to walk up a set of steps, across a platform, and back down. I had on this cap and gown. When they called my name, I was thinking, With all this attention, I don't want to trip. I just wanted to make sure I could stick my hand out to receive it and not fall on my face. No cosmic thoughts. Just very, very micro.

There was applause for every student. When they called my name, there were a few claps in the audience, probably from my family. Mostly there was this silence. It was eerie, quiet. But it was as if none of that mattered. I think the fact that it was so silent was indicative of the fact that I had done something. And really all nine of us had. Even though I was the one receiving the diploma, I couldn't have done it without the support of the others.

Afterward I went to where my mother, my aunt, and my brother were. Dr. Martin Luther King was sitting with my family. I knew he was speaking in Pine Bluff at the black college, but I didn't know he was going to come up to Little Rock for my graduation. I had never met him before that. He had a plane to catch, so we just spent a brief period of time together.

At this point, I'm a high school graduate of sixteen. I've gotten a load off of my shoulders, and I clearly was not interested in cosmic issues. I wanted to go meet my friends. We were having a party over at the house and celebrating.

I had the broader view a few days before. I remember reading in the paper that my graduating was going to be a real milestone. I thought to myself, This is great, but I want to do something else in life besides graduating from Little Rock Central High School. What do I do from here?

Little Rock, I think, became symbolic for a lot of things. It was one of the most televised of the desegregation cases. It was made for TV. It was good and evil. It was about as black and white as you could make life. You had nine kids who were innocent enough they couldn't have harmed a lot of people, and you had Governor Faubus playing the heavy. You had real drama.

One thing that I think is very important is this:

while the nine of us may have been preselected, there really are nine, ten, thirty, forty, fifty kids in every community that could have done that. It wasn't that nine people fell out of the sky in Little Rock. We were all ordinary kids. You really do have the ability to do a lot more than either you've been told or you've been led to believe by your surroundings. If given the opportunity, you'd be surprised at how much you can do, how much you can achieve.

ARLAM CARR

Arlam Carr was about to enter high school when he and his parents sued the Montgomery school system, challenging the segregation laws. This was 1964, ten years after the Supreme Court decision in the Brown case, and seven years after the Little Rock Nine integrated Central High School.

I remember being very young and going by Lanier High School. I didn't understand it was a high school. I just knew it was a school and that it looked pretty. I told my mother I wanted to go to that school. She didn't say anything then. I guess it was hard for her to actually tell a child who's four or five, "You can't go to that school because you're black."

After the school integration in Little Rock, they started integrating in different places. In Montgomery, attorney Fred Gray was trying to get people to bring a lawsuit to integrate the whole school system. When I was in the eighth grade, my mother said we would do it. Another lady who had a son also agreed. There was a Methodist minister who had a lot of kids. He was going to be a part of it too. When word came out that the suit was going to be filed to integrate the schools, the Methodist church very abruptly moved that minister to Mississippi. I mean, snap, just like that.

After they moved the minister, the other lady became nervous and said she didn't want to participate. That left us. My mom asked me if I still wanted to do it. I said, "Can I go to Lanier if I do it?"

She said, "Yes."

So I said, "Let's do it."

The suit was filed on a Thursday. On that Friday, they had a big article in the paper with my name and address, who my parents were—the whole works. There had been bombings of churches and homes in Montgomery. A lot of friends called my mother and said they could come over and guard our house. My mother told them, "No."

That Friday night after the lawsuit was filed, we started getting phone calls. People would say ugly things, or hang up. My mother said, "I'm going to watch the news until 10:30, and then I'm going to take the phone off the hook. When I get up, I'll put it back on, but I'm not going to get up all night long and answer the phone."

The only thing we did was my parents moved into my bedroom because their bedroom was right on the corner. My mother said, "If something happens, it happens. I'm just going to put it in the hands of the Lord."

That was 1964, the year after President Kennedy was killed, and the lawsuit was *Arlam Carr v. Montgomery County Board of Education*. I was the lead plaintiff. The suit was to desegregate the schools so we could go to whatever school we wanted. When the ruling came down, we won. I felt good.

Judge Frank M. Johnson ruled that for the first year, only the first, tenth, eleventh, and twelfth grades would be integrated, and the next year, all of the grades. I was going into the ninth grade in the fall of 1964, so I didn't go that first year. I went in 1965 in the tenth grade.

The year I started at Lanier, the school system said they didn't want us to come the first day. There were thirteen of us. They told us to come the second day after classes started. We went to the principal's office, and they divided us up into groups and walked us to our homerooms. We were all in separate classes. We waited until one person in the group went into a class. Then we'd go to the next class. I was the last.

You know how kids are the first days of school—talking a lot, making noise. I was standing outside the door of my class where the kids couldn't see me. The principal called the teacher to the door and said, "He's going to be in your homeroom." When I stepped around the corner and the kids saw me, you could have heard a pin drop. The noise was cut just like that.

I'll never forget how you could be walking down the hall, and they'd just part. The first time I was a little intimidated, but then I felt like a king—everybody's parting the waters for the black kids. That's fine with me. Got no problem with that.

After a while their attitude was, "Well, they're here, we gotta accept them. We got to go to school, so let's make the best of it." At first the kids that I tended to get friendly with had parents at Maxwell

Air Force base. They had lived in different parts of the country and had been around black kids.

Senior year I asked this white guy if he'd sign my yearbook. I had known him from the tenth grade on, and we had become pretty good friends. He wrote that at one time he had been a bigot and had hated black people. Now he realized that people are people, black or white. Meeting me and knowing me had changed him. He ended it by saying, "We shall overcome."

DELORES BOYD

Delores Boyd was one of the thirteen students with Arlam Carr who integrated Lanier High School in Montgomery in 1965.

By the time I left junior high school, I was more than ready to be in the group to go to the desegregated schools. I knew that white students at public schools were taking Latin, French, and Spanish. I knew that no black student had that. I knew that at some schools white students were taking sciences that were not offered to us. And I wanted to go to the best high school.

I can't remember having a big powwow with my family. It just seemed natural. There was no doubt in my mind that I would go when it was time for high school. And that was 1965.

My memory of that first year comes in bunches. I remember my history teacher. I knew she despised me. She never would say "Negro." She would always look at me directly and say "nigger" or "nigra." It was almost as if she dared me to say something about it. What was there to say? She was a mean old woman who grudgingly gave me an A.

Nobody would sit behind me in biology class. I know that was typical because the black students compared notes. Teachers would let the white kids sit where they wanted. The kids would just move their chairs to distance themselves from me. Nobody would ever sit behind me, unless it was a classroom with a teacher who required seating alphabetically. My English teacher was like that, and I salute her to this day. She was the fairest teacher I had. Everybody had to sit alphabetically, so no one could run away from me.

That type of taunting was almost expected in light of [Alabama governor] George Wallace. I mean, here's a man running around the country saying, "Segregation now and forever," and that he'd stand in the schoolhouse doors to block integration. He became the symbol of resistance, and he was here in Montgomery, the capital.

There were the overt racists in school, who took delight in taunting you. In the hall they'd be the ones who'd say "nigger this" or laugh or do things that were just dirty. Then there were those who chose to pretend you were not there. Their form of racism was as painful. They would almost make you feel like you had some disease. They'd never say anything, just ignore you.

Then there was a group, primarily of the Jewish kids and some Maxwell Air Force base kids, who were sensitive and courageous. There weren't many Jewish kids, but I remember most of their names. They were the ones who'd try to be conversational. They wouldn't participate in the taunts, and occasionally one would sit with you at lunch. That was unusual because typically the lunchroom experience was solitary.

The only physical incident that happened to me was at lunch. Somebody threw a carton of chocolate milk at me. Struck me right on my head. What do you do? You just clean yourself up and go on.

I guess I had been conditioned to believe that struggle was just a part of the process. And that there were people out there who would make it difficult for us. We were constantly told, "Keep your mind on your study, don't fight back. Just leave them alone."

I've always thought that children, black and white, have a much better basis for overcoming racism than adults. But white children back then had been told by their parents to expect the worst of us. They'd been told by the governor, by the mayor, by all these folk in power. They knew nothing about black folk. They thought we were monkeys from Africa for sure. All they knew came from the media and the fools who were in leadership. It was just a hot climate.

The first year was the worst year, but it didn't even take all year to get over the hump. I think the teachers realized that we weren't dumb, or if we were, we were no dumber than whites. Grudgingly, many of them were surprised to know that we were bright. And students realized that we were bright. That was very surprising to them, and some of them eased up. Some never did.

I don't count a whole bunch of friends, but I never was that much on socializing. We weren't into going over there to be liked. That's why I didn't get all uptight about it. I went there to do as well as I could and go to the next stage. I wanted to be a lawyer. I thought that Lanier could give me a better foundation than a poorly funded segregated school.

Going to Lanier removed this mystique about white being better. I had been told by teachers at the black junior high that you are as good as they are. But when I got to Lanier, I realized I shouldn't make white people my standard. It's not that we're looking for association because we think association makes us as good as they are. It's that there are opportunities here that we are not being given.

Twenty years after Delores graduated from Lanier, she was told a story she had never heard before about her class standing at graduation.

I know a black woman who teaches at a trade school here. She recently told me something I didn't know. I had gone to speak to her class, and she was walking me to my car afterwards. She told me about a certain white teacher from Lanier she had seen. The white teacher mentioned my name and said to my friend, "Something has haunted me for a long time. Delores Boyd should have been valedictorian of her class. But we just couldn't believe a black child could be that smart, and that's why she wasn't."

I told my best friend the story, and she got all upset and angry for me and wondered why I wasn't angry and bitter. I said, "Well, in the first place, I don't know if it's true or not. I did graduate in the top ten percent, but I never looked for standings. I never asked anybody how the valedictorian was chosen. And most of the teachers were fair in grading. It's possible, but that's over twenty years ago, and why should it anger me now? Lots of things were done, I'm sure, that were like that."

THELMA EUBANKS

In 1966, Thelma Eubanks and a friend were the first black students to graduate from Gibson High School (now called McComb) in McComb, Mississippi.

I had heard that the other schools around here maybe would be integrated, so I said, "Hey, you all, how about us going to Gibson?" I talked two of my brothers and a couple of friends into going. I was a senior. There were seven of us that first year—four seniors, two sophomores, and a junior. We had a hard time that year. My friend Marionette and my brother used to fuss at me 'cause my big mouth was the one that talked them into going.

The first day all of the white people parked around the school. I remember seeing a couple of police cars, but they were across the street. Everybody was scared. I think Bernell was walking first. He asked Marionette if she was scared. She told him, "I'm so scared my knees feel like they're going to buckle under." All of the white kids were standing around the front of the school, looking. So I said, "I'll go first." I didn't let them know my knees were wobbling too.

Then we went in the gym. Some of the whites were in groups saying, "I smell a nigger, I smell a nigger." That's all you heard all the way till you went in and sat down.

We had so many prejudiced teachers who didn't want the schools to be integrated. Like my history teacher. She wouldn't come right out and say we didn't have any business coming over there. She'd say, "People ought to stay in their own place." She would say that in class, and I was the only black in class.

Going there made me realize how unequal the schools were. Stuff they had had in the seventh and eighth grades, we were just getting as juniors and seniors at the black school. I had had French 1 at the black school, but at the black school all you had to do was learn to count from one to twenty and to say the alphabet. Got over here and they were conjugating verbs. I mean, they could read the stuff like they were reading English. It took me a whole lot of catching up. But I got so I could read before I got out of that class.

We had homework every day. Shoot, we maybe had homework once a week at the black school. We weren't used to that. Sometimes we wouldn't get through until it was time to take a bath and go to bed. The white kids were used to it because that was a good school.

Barbara Lee's mother lost her job. The lady that Barbara's mother was working for was our P.E. teacher. Now, she was real prejudiced, you could tell. When she found out Barbara was going to McComb, she fired her mama from cleaning her house. Barbara took a lot of heat, but she was the smartest of all of us, bookwise.

I was baby-sitting for a white lady for her little girl, who was about three years old. Her son was in the tenth grade, and I went to a French class with him. He was asking me one evening had I got out my homework. His mom just looked at him. She didn't say anything then, but I heard her talking to him after I had left the den and was back in the kitchen. Then she told me she wasn't going to be needing my services anymore.

In school no matter what kind of locks we got for our lockers, the white kids always knew the combination or could find the key to open it. Maybe because their dads owned all the businesses. Bernice had a big pile of dog stuff put on top of her books one day. She was reaching up to get a book, and she ended up sticking her hand in it. She went to the principal and told him about it. He wanted her to clean it out. She told him she wasn't going to clean it out because she didn't put it there. He finally made the janitor do it.

Two girls you'd occasionally see smiling at you, but they wouldn't let their friends see them do it. I think those were the only two who tried to be friendly. The rest of them were standoffish. They called us "nigger" almost for the entire year. I tell you, we went through something that year. Two of the black students didn't graduate. They had to go to summer school.

Sometimes I hated myself for doing it because it cut out all of our social life that last year. We couldn't be in any of the extracurricular activities. No kind of clubs, no sports, nothing. All the blacks had to stay in homeroom while everybody was going to clubs.

But I *am* glad I did it. By graduation things had gotten lighter. We were the first two blacks to graduate from Gibson High, and we weren't going to miss the graduation ceremony after that hard fight. We had made it! It was light and easy. A lot of blacks were in the audience. Some of them we didn't even know.

They were just coming because they knew blacks attended there. It was lively.

I got a very hard handshake from the superintendent and the principal. I remember, they shook my hand like they were glad it was done.

*A freedom bus burning
outside Anniston, Alabama.*

4. *Sit-ins, Freedom Rides, and Other Protests*

THE SIT-INS AND OTHER PROTESTS

After the bus boycott in Montgomery, many of the early civil rights protests took place in Birmingham under the courageous leadership of activist Reverend

Fred Shuttlesworth, pastor of the Bethel Baptist Church. When Alabama state officials banned the NAACP in June 1956, Reverend Shuttlesworth organized the Alabama Christian Movement for Human Rights (ACMHR). The ACMHR sponsored many events to integrate city facilities. Segregationist reaction was violent. So many black churches and homes were bombed that the city was sometimes called "Bombingham," with one particular black area known as "Dynamite Hill."

Birmingham Police Commissioner Eugene "Bull" Connor was a rabid segregationist who took every opportunity to arrest civil rights protesters. But the racist violence and the complicity of the local police did not stop Reverend Shuttlesworth, who continued to organize protest actions throughout the fifties.

Although these demonstrations had been taking place in Birmingham, the civil rights movement as a whole did not become widespread and receive extensive national attention until the full-scale student sit-ins began in 1960. On February 1, four black college freshmen in Greensboro, North Carolina, went to a local Woolworth's store and bought some supplies. But when they sat down at the "white" lunch counter, they were told they wouldn't be served. If their money was "good enough" to pay for supplies, they argued, it should be accepted for food as well. They remained seated at the counter until closing time, never having been served.

News of their protest action spread rapidly to other schools. Within weeks, students were sitting-in at lunch counters in cities throughout the South. Sympathy protests also were held in northern cities. At a Woolworth's store in Boston, Massachusetts, for example, where blacks *were* allowed to sit at the lunch counters, protesters nevertheless marched outside, asking people not to shop there until Woolworth's ended segregation in its southern stores.

On Easter weekend 1960 more than a hundred students met at Shaw University in Raleigh, North Carolina. Encouraged and inspired by SCLC worker Ella Baker, they formed a student organization to coordinate the sit-ins and other civil rights activities. It was called the Student Nonviolent Coordinating Committee (SNCC, pronounced "snick"). SNCC became a major organizer of civil rights activities in the South in the sixties.

Civil rights demonstrators believed that racist laws should be disobeyed and challenged. And they were willing to go to jail for their beliefs. "In order to change the law, we had to break the law, and that's one thing I knew," says Ricky Shuttlesworth. "The only way you could change things was to demonstrate."

And so the demonstrations expanded beyond lunch counter sit-ins. Protesters had wade-ins at segregated pools, kneel-ins at all-white churches, sit-ins at segregated movie theaters—protests at most every kind of public place. Fred Taylor, for example, went with a group to a sit-in at the Montgomery public library. Although today it is difficult to imagine, in the 1960s blacks were not allowed in the library. "Their argument," he says, "was that we needed a library card. But they refused to grant us permission to apply for the card." That discriminatory policy "was the basis for the court challenge that led to desegregation of the library."

The civil rights movement was based on the idea of nonviolent direct action. This meant taking to the streets to confront discriminatory barriers, but doing it without any use of force. The Nashville Student Movement, headed by Diane Nash, was one of the most influential of the student groups. The Nashville students had been trained at weekly workshops in nonviolence led by divinity student James Lawson. It took courage and strength, they learned, not to use force to accomplish their goals, not to strike back, but rather to try to convince people of the justice of their protest by the way they expressed their ideas and by their behavior.

Larry Russell from Birmingham sums it up: "I was always trained that if you're hit, you hit back. But this was one occasion where we united under the idea and philosophy of nonviolence. We didn't feel that violence was the way to get the job done."

It wasn't always easy to be nonviolent. Towanner Hinkle in Selma, Alabama, says:

Dr. King and the others always told us, "Don't fight, just leave peacefully." Very hard to do, though. When people start saying, "Nigger get out of here"—very, very hard to accept it, but we went on. We could have started a fight because there was enough of us to really tear the town down, but we tried to be peaceful. We accepted it because we wanted to do what Dr. King asked us to do, be nonviolent.

At first we thought nonviolence was the worst thing. We thought maybe if we could fight, if we could just burn something down, it would help improve things. But after going to mass meetings and mass meetings and mass meetings, we learned that what he was telling us was right because they would have hurt us.

Mary Gadson in Birmingham describes how the protesters were taught. "They trained you to be disciplined. They would get up into your face and say all kinds of things, like 'Nigger sit down!' and 'Nigger move!' You'd have to stand there and take it. You were being disciplined to take the harshness. The training was to take control. I wouldn't let them get to me. I would not allow the person who was doing the shouting to be in control."

If someone was unable or unwilling to agree to be nonviolent, they were not allowed to participate in demonstrations. But as Ricky Shuttlesworth notes, the movement was big enough to find a place for most everyone. "They could do calling or writing letters or something else. They weren't looked down upon, because there was so much to do. They always needed workers to do something."

From 1960 until 1965, scarcely a day went by without a nonviolent protest in some southern city or town. Some actions were broad-based marches and demonstrations, protesting against widespread patterns of segregation in a city or town. Other actions were specific and limited to one place. The stories in this chapter reflect that wide spectrum of protest.

FRANCES FOSTER

Frances Foster was best friends with Ricky Shuttlesworth and was involved in the early Birmingham protest actions of the 1950s as well as the demonstrations in the 1960s.

* * *

I went over to Ricky's house, and Reverend Shuttlesworth asked me, "Frances, you think you want to get involved?"

I said, "Yes sir."

I remember my first demonstration. It was eight days after my fourteenth birthday. I had on the clothes I got for my birthday that year. My aunt saw me on the television and she told my mother, "Bea, that girl's on TV with her new dress on and her new kid shoes and that new purse you bought her."

Everybody chose the store that they wanted to go to. There were possibly a dozen of us. Before we went, we had prayer, and that gave us confidence. Some went to Loveman's or Newberry's. I went to Pitzitz with my partner. I bought books. After I made the purchase, I went to the luncheonette on the mezzanine and sat down. There was a young black lady working there. She was afraid to come over to the table because she didn't want to lose her job, or do anything detrimental to herself. Or perhaps she thought something would happen to me.

A white lady came over and said, "What are you doing up here? You know you can't eat up here."

I said, "Why can't I? I made a purchase here in the store and they accepted my money for that. I'd like to order, please."

She repeated, "You have to go. You just can't eat up here. You know better."

I said, "I'm not leaving until I'm served," and so I sat there.

A white man came up and said, "I'm going to have to ask you to get out of here, girl. You know you all supposed to go downstairs somewhere."

I said, "I'd like to have a menu, please. Will you have someone come clean the table off."

A few minutes later television cameras and the Birmingham police came. "Girl, you know you ain't supposed to be up here. Come on, let's go. We're going to take you on down to jail."

I said, "I'm still waiting to be served my lunch. They haven't come to clean the table off yet, and I'd like to order."

The policeman said, "You know ain't no niggers allowed to eat up here." The cameras were right there, so I politely came down the steps like the young lady I was at that time.

I wasn't afraid at all. I was very happy that day because I felt like I was gaining something. I felt I had done something for myself and my race. I knew it would be televised, so my purpose was fulfilled. We went there to show the world what they were doing to us here in Birmingham.

Downstairs they had cars waiting for us. [Police Commissioner] Bull Connor was there. When I got down, there were about six people in the car already. He told me to get in. I said, "That car is too crowded. I can't get in the car and wrinkle up my dress." It was my new dress.

He said, "Heifer, if you don't get in this car, I'll take this gun and hit you upside your head."

I said, "I'm not a heifer and I'm not going to get in that car. There's no seat for me to sit down, and I can't wrinkle up my dress." Back and forth like that we went. Finally he made somebody sit on somebody else's lap, and I got in.

They took us straight to juvenile. In jail they let us watch it on television. I was so proud of what I had done. I knew that one day segregation had to go away.

* * *

JAMES ROBERSON

As a college student, James Roberson helped organize the first sit-ins in Huntsville, Alabama, in 1960.

I had been in the struggle—that was one of Reverend Shuttlesworth's words—all the way through, and at sixteen I went off to college in Huntsville. A guy named Hank worked for SNCC, and he had been given my name. Hank came to my dormitory room and asked me if I was in the movement. I said, "Yes." When he said we needed to get something started in Huntsville, I agreed. We were not the only ones organizing. Students were doing this at other schools. Hank was our source of information about what was going on elsewhere.

At that time I was president of my freshman class. We had a meeting in the basement of the First Baptist Church. We decided to target fast-food places. We had classes on what to do and what not to do. Number one, stay alert. Number two, the object of the sit-in was to take control of the counters. Taking control meant to occupy all the seats. This would eliminate money coming in, and that would create a confrontation. The main thing was not to be vulgar. Do not curse, do not exchange insults, sit quietly. Believe it or not, whites thought it was an insult to sit near a black. If a black sat down next to a white, the white would jump up instantly.

The first place we went to was Shoney's Big Boy. This was the first time anything had ever been done in Huntsville. We planned not to get arrested. We were to go in, demand food, and when they called the policemen, leave and go somewhere else.

We were very well dressed. They weren't going to be able to say we were not clean. We were not drinking, we didn't smell, we were not hostile. It was a weekend night, and the place was filled almost to capacity with whites. As we walked in, there was the clacking and clicking of plates and forks. Snap, poof, it stopped suddenly. It was like some people from Mars had walked in. Nobody would seat us. The five of us just stood there. The silence captivated the whole restaurant. You would have thought we had walked in nude, or had three eyes. We waited a long minute. The kind of minute where you can feel your skin tightening up and ants biting. You knew you were doing something "wrong." We were not afraid, but we were tense because we didn't know if they were going to start a fight.

Then one of the white patrons said, "You get the tar and I'll get the feathers. We'll get these niggers out of here." We all turned around and looked at him. He quieted down. We had no weapons—no knives, no guns, no sticks. We were not going to get arrested for carrying concealed weapons.

The manager was a young white guy. "I can't serve you," he said. "I'm from up North and I understand, but you guys just can't eat here." We told him we weren't going to leave until we ate. He said he'd have to call the police. We said, "Do what you have to do, but we're not leaving." By the time he hung up the phone, we said we'd be back and we quietly walked off, got in the car, and went down to another place. The Huntsville police were going everywhere that night, saying, "What's going on?"

We went to another place and sat at the counter. This black guy in his forties was mopping the floor. He was so proud of us sitting there, he was just beaming over. Of course the manager was white. There were no black managers then. The manager said, "You all gonna have to get up." We didn't say anything. So he turned to the black guy standing by his bucket and said, "Throw it on them! Throw it on them!"

The guy hesitated. The manager yelled, "Doggone it, throw it!" The guy tried not to throw it on us. He threw the water down the counter. Then he walked off. I never will forget his eyes. You could see the hurt, the plea for understanding and forgiveness. You could see him thinking, I had to do it. I go along with what you all are doing, but I got a family to feed. I got bills to pay and I'm under the control of this man. If I don't, I'm going to lose it all. So he did it and walked away. You could see he was crushed. We just sat there.

BARBARA HOWARD

In Montgomery, after the bus boycott, the Montgomery Improvement Association (MIA) sponsored other civil rights activities in the early 1960s. For Barbara Howard, the eighth and ninth grades were the time of sit-ins.

I was one of the first to integrate a movie theater. I remember that evening. The MIA put us in pairs, two to the Paramount and two to the Empire. I integrated the Empire theater. They did not let us in the first time we tried. We went back a week later, and then they let us in. I remember sitting in the center aisle, scared to death. Fortunately, there weren't many whites there. I remember that distinctly. But boy, we did not stay for the entire movie—I remember that much too. It was the symbolic entering, integration, of the place. I was so scared, I don't remember what the movie was.

What if an older redneck did something to us, then how would we respond? We had been taught if you had to speak, let it be something polite. No cursing. If they struck you, we were told how to crouch and protect ourselves. No fighting back. Would I be able to do what we'd been taught? That was the fear.

Nonviolence was the philosophy that was being taught to all of us in the movement, stemming from Dr. King's dream of an integrated society and his agreement with Mahatma Gandhi from India. We did freedom workshops at some of the churches, where they would teach us how to act, what to say, how to protect ourselves. Songs—that was the key, that was the spirit lifter. "Ain't Gonna Let Nobody Turn Me 'Round." "We Shall Overcome," of course, and "O Freedom." One of my favorites was "Go Tell It on the Mountain." This was during George Wallace's time, and Bull Connor, so we put their names in the songs.

A lot of times we would go into the apartment buildings to recruit young people. Many of our rallies were not scheduled in churches, but were in open areas. We'd recruit young people to join us for the sit-ins.

"You can't sit back at your home and think that white people are going to give you something," we'd say. "They are not. You gotta come on out and join us and take it. Help make a difference." We would tell them that we were trying to integrate, to make all of what's available to the whites available to us.

At one point we started saying "black." "Black is

beautiful.'' I can remember the student leader Stokely Carmichael coming up with that slogan. It made us start to appreciate our own color. It built our self-awareness.

RICKY SHUTTLESWORTH

In 1960 Ricky and her sister and brother, Pat and Fred, Jr., spent part of the summer at the integrated Highlander Folk School in Tennessee. On their return trip to Birmingham, they were arrested when they "sat-in" in the front of the bus and refused to move.

Highlander was an interracial camp, and I think we were there six weeks. It was an experiment of children from various nationalities and races living together. Oh, I liked it! We had groups divided into cabins for various activities. We swam. We had creative writing. I remember one little song that we made up, a non-sense opera that we put to music.

That summer was the most fun I have ever had in my life. The cabins were completely racially mixed. It was also the first time I ever met an atheist. His name was Roger. One day it was real hot. Roger put his fist up to the sky and said, "Rain, you bastard!" Clap! Lightning happened, and everybody ran. I don't know if we ran because he was cursing God or because of the lightning.

When we left the camp to go home, we got on an interstate bus in Tennessee headed to Birmingham. We sat in the front. At home we had been doing bus demonstrations. We just wouldn't sit in the back of even a school bus. We weren't making any noise or anything. By the time we got to Gadsden, Alabama, all of a sudden there were these police cars. The bus driver came and told us to get up and move to the back. One of us said, "We don't have to. This is an interstate bus."

Then policemen came to bodily take us off. They were mean policemen. I had had so much fun at camp, I was hoarse from all the singing and laughing and shouting. At the police station I was talking, and evidently the policeman couldn't hear me because I was so hoarse. He slapped me. My brother reached for him, and they grabbed him to restrain him.

The police took all our memorabilia—photographs and papers, all the addresses from people we'd met. We had had such a good time. It's sad that the police took all of that. Out of all that they did to us, that was the worst.

We were in jail overnight. Pat and I were in a lady's cell. Fred was directly under us, and he sang all night long. We had been singing softly on the bus. I think he sang to let us know that he was okay.

The food was horrible. It was fried dried bologna and grits with grease. The toilet was an open bowl with the worst smell. I was afraid, but I was mostly hurt that they took my stuff, all the plays, the poems, and the pictures. At that camp they had made us realize that you are somebody and you can use your mind and develop. And the police took everything.

GLADIS WILLIAMS

Gladis Williams was a high school student during the Montgomery movement of the 1960s.

* * *

At the doctor, we had separate waiting rooms, one for the colored, one for the white. The colored room was smaller, and was in worse shape than the white room. I was thirteen or fourteen. My sister, Lula, and I challenged that. We said okay, we're going to the white room. They had a black nurse for the blacks and a white nurse for the whites. The white nurse came over and told us we had to get out of there. She got the doctor. He called my mama and told her, "Look, don't never bring them back down here no more." And that was that. We didn't go back.

We would go after school to the MIA office, and we would organize. First of all we would find out who was going to what store. Girl/boy, girl/boy. Nobody went by themselves. We would always have a mixed group. We'd get the names, telephones, addresses of next of kin for the different people who were going.

Usually we would have a nice little rally before we'd go. We would talk to the Lord. Everybody was very close to the Lord. We would have a prayer. Got to have a prayer before we go to do battle. And we would get out the picket signs.

Kress's and H. L. Green were segregated. By the time we'd get down there, usually the police was waiting on us. Let's say a group of six was picketing in front of H. L. Green, or going to sit-in at the counters. The first group would go in, and we'd see what happened to them. If they got arrested, we'd have another group come in. Then they'd get arrested. And all of a sudden everybody would end up in jail.

Don't even ask me how many times I was arrested! They arrested us for unlawful assembly and demonstrating without a permit. They would get us for disorderly conduct, or disturbing the peace, even though we were very orderly.

They would take you to jail after they read you the riot act. If you were a juvenile, you were supposed to go to Juvenile Hall, but usually if you were a demonstrator or picketer, you'd go where everybody else went, to the old city jail.

Going to jail, oh, it was a badge of honor during that time! When you demonstrated, you already knew it's possible you're going to jail. It's possible you're gonna get hurt. It's possible you're gonna get killed. But our minds were made up. We had an understanding with the Lord that this is what we wanted to do. And He was always out there with us. So as far as having fear, we didn't even know what fear was. We just had our minds set on freedom, and that was it.

When I became twenty-one, I *ran* down to the poll and registered. It was the proudest day of my life. Oh, I was excited. After working so hard on different voter registration drives, literally pulling people off the street to register to vote—hey, I was so proud, I didn't know what to do when my time came.

I still vote. Oh God, I wouldn't miss it. A lot of progress has taken place. And we helped make a lot of the changes here in Montgomery. All kinds of changes—jobs, education, housing, voting.

I have no regrets. None whatsoever. Everything we did back during the civil rights movement was from the heart. You know how some people holler, "Where's my fame?" I don't look for that. I got mine. I got mine. It's like Dr. King said. If you haven't found something worth fighting for, then you ain't fit to live anyway. You got to have something that makes it worth it.

THE FREEDOM RIDES

The Freedom Rides were among the most famous of the civil rights protests. The Supreme Court had ruled that buses traveling interstate could not be segregated; nor could waiting rooms and restaurants that served interstate bus passengers. Although in this instance United States law was on the side of the protesters, most southern states ignored these laws. James Farmer, head of CORE, called for a "Freedom Ride" to force southern states to obey the Court rulings. On May 4, 1961, thirteen people, seven blacks and six whites, left Washington, D.C., on buses headed for New Orleans, Louisiana. They sat wherever they wanted on the bus and planned to use all the local facilities along the way.

Just outside Anniston, Alabama, some fifty miles from Birmingham, an armed mob of segregationists fire-bombed the first bus and beat several of the fleeing passengers. The second bus was surrounded by a raging mob at the Birmingham passenger terminal. Some of the riders were beaten so badly they suffered permanent physical damage. In a report to the Federal Bureau of Investigation (FBI), an informant stated that Birmingham's police commissioner, Eugene "Bull" Connor, had agreed to give the mob fifteen minutes before he sent in the police. News coverage of the brutal attacks on the Freedom Riders horrified the American public. The attacks took place on Mother's Day and became known as the "Mother's Day Massacre."

After the attacks in Anniston and Birmingham, the Freedom Riders decided to end the bus trip and fly to New Orleans instead. But a group of young people, mostly college students, believed that the Freedom

Rides should continue. Diane Nash, head of the Nashville Student Movement, said that if the Freedom Riders were stopped "as a result of violence . . . the future of the movement was going to be cut short." The students argued that integrated groups of passengers had to travel through the South until the system of segregation was broken. From a pool of volunteers, Nash carefully chose a new group of students to continue the rides. They all discussed the grave risk of physical danger, possibly death, that lay ahead.

At first no bus driver was willing to continue the trip from Birmingham to Montgomery, Alabama. Finally, with pressure from United States Attorney General Robert Kennedy, the governor of Alabama agreed to provide state police protection on the route between the two cities. When the bus arrived in Montgomery, however, all police protection vanished, and the riders were viciously assaulted by segregationists at the bus station.

The next night a mass meeting was held at First Baptist Church in Montgomery. A screaming white mob surrounded the church, trapping those inside. Federal marshals and the Alabama National Guard finally arrived to disperse the mob in the early morning hours, preventing massive bloodshed.

The Freedom Rides continued throughout the summer of 1961. In Jackson, Mississippi, integrated groups of riders were routinely arrested for violating the local segregation laws at the bus station, and sent to prison. Finally in September the United States government issued additional regulations regarding integration at interstate bus stations, and the arrests stopped. The Freedom Riders had won.

Thereafter civil rights workers throughout the

South were often called Freedom Riders, regardless of the particular projects they worked on. In fact, the term became a badge of honor in the movement.

JAMES ROBERSON

James Roberson was seventeen years old when the Freedom Riders came through Birmingham.

It was in the afternoon when they started bringing the Freedom Riders to Bethel Church. White kids and black kids had been beaten. That was the first time I saw human blood being spilled for the cause. I actually saw people hurt and scared. They were holding handkerchiefs to their heads to stop the bleeding.

These kids weren't too much older than I. They were college kids. I knew that the police would beat up black people, so that was nothing unusual for me. But white people beating up white folks . . . I did not believe a white would do that to their own kind. You have to realize the mind-set of a black from the South—white folks all stick together. Yet these were their own people they were beating up!

I saw that they were bleeding just like we were bleeding. I realized then the connection was not racial. To see the inhumane treatment of their own made me realize it was not the color of the skin, but the principle they believed in.

RICKY SHUTTLESWORTH

Many of the Freedom Riders who had been attacked outside of Anniston and in Birmingham

*were brought to the Shuttlesworth home. Ricky
was sixteen years old at the time.*

I could tell when something was going on because
our phone always rang. I had heard that these young
people were coming down to the test the system. They
expected trouble. I was excited that something was
going to happen, yet fearful because we knew the
wrath of the southerners.

When the Freedom Riders came through, they
brought Jim Peck to our house. We had a guest room,
and my mother had a beautiful white bedspread in
there. They laid him on that spread. He was so bloody,
we never were able to use any of that bedding again.
I had been involved in a lot of things, but I hadn't
seen that much blood anywhere at any one time.

My mother had a degree in teaching and in nursing,
and she ministered to him. Here was a man whose
dad had to be rich since he owned the Peck and Peck
department store. And he would give up perhaps his
life to come and do this for me. I had a lot of respect
for him. I don't know if I said anything to him. I
might have brought Mother something to help her. I
just really admired his courage for coming to help us.

JOSEPH LACEY

*Joe Lacey witnessed the attack on the Freedom
Riders in Montgomery.*

On that Saturday morning down at the bus station, I
was with a bunch of college kids. I was a freshman.
We went down there when we heard the bus was coming in. We saw the mob attack the bus. I was in the
crowd of persons who were beaten. Although I was

not hurt, I was mashed up against a building getting away from the mobs.

The troopers withdrew from the scene. The city police withdrew from the scene. The county sheriff withdrew from the scene. Colonel Floyd Mann [Alabama public safety director and head of the state highway patrol] was the only officer who stayed there, and he enforced the law as a professional. I saw him personally step into that mob with his pistol and force them to back off.

I saw the Freedom Riders beaten. I cried. I just couldn't believe it. Human beings beating other human beings like that. I mean, they were beating them viciously. One particular guy, who was a short, cigar-smoking, potbellied guy, a salesman at one of our local car dealerships, beat people like he was going crazy.

At that time we didn't have ambulance companies like we have now. Funeral homes did ambulance service. The white ambulances would not go. I was talking to a schoolmate of mine, and he told me that his dad was driving that day to help pick people up. They tried to go in there and the bricks hit them. Finally the ambulances were allowed to come through. Blood was flowing down there like some of those Civil War battles.

About four of us who were college kids were watching it and shaking our heads with disgust. The crowd dispersed after the beating. I went directly home and got on my typewriter and wrote President John Kennedy, begging him for help, telling him how bad it was here. I had never seen it that vicious before. I never got an answer, but the next night when the federal marshals held the crowd back at the [First Baptist] church, that more than paid for it.

That next night I was in the church. It was inde-
scribable. President Kennedy had sent in about four
to five hundred U.S. marshals who were supposed to
enforce the law because the city police had completely
abdicated. I can remember seeing these marshals
transported from Maxwell Air Force base in postal
vehicles. They ringed the church. Looking out the
window, you could see the postal vehicles all up the
street.

The church was packed. I would say fifteen hundred to two thousand people. When we started chanting those songs, you just got together and started
singing and rocking with the wave. It was something
to behold. Never in history has a group ever stuck
together like that.

All of a sudden you could hear the crowd outside
getting louder and louder. You could hear bricks hitting the building. They were screaming, "Kill the niggers! Bring them out, bring them out! Let's go in and
get them out!" We had a little recreation room and
we had baseball bats downstairs. So a bunch of us
were going to grab some bats, but the older people
said, "Put them down!"

The telephone service at the church was on and off.
The wires were interrupted. Someone said, "How are
we going to get a message out?" I remembered having muscled my way into church once or twice for
choir rehearsal. So I went out the side window. There
was a drop of about twenty-five feet. I jumped back
on a little retaining wall on the side of the church and
went behind the houses and through the block to my
grandmother's house and made phone calls for Reverend Abernathy and some parents who were concerned about the safety of their people. And I made
some calls for other people who wanted their families

to know where they were. I went in and out of the church that night. Only the Reverend and some other people knew I was going in and out. The mob was in the front of the church. I slipped in between the houses. If they had had somebody back there, they would have definitely had me.

The crowd outside would surge forward, and they were throwing bricks and everything. Some of our windows were broken, and the tear gas seeped into the church. I remember the tear gas, and how the fumes came in and hurt our eyes. The marshals had cordoned the church off and were repelling the crowd. Some of these marshals were really hurt by the bricks that were thrown. One or two marshals were, I think, damaged for life. I can only say this: those marshals prevented a massive bloodshed that night. If that mob had gotten into the church, it would have been just . . . there would have been many lives lost, many lives.

GWENDOLYN PATTON

Gwen Patton was a student when the Freedom Riders came through Montgomery.

The key in the sixties for me as a young person was the Freedom Riders. When they arrived in Montgomery in May 1961, I wanted to go down to the bus station. We heard on the radio that people were being beaten up—chains, baseball bats, all kinds of stuff. I thought it was important for me to go, but my aunt Chick, who I was staying with, did not participate much in civil rights activity. So I got mad at her because she had the car and would not take me down to the station.

Two or three days later we had a mass meeting, and some of the Freedom Riders came. I brought some of them back to my aunt Chick's house. We were sitting in the living room when my aunt came through the door. She was just outraged. She said, "Gwendolyn, come to the kitchen with me." Then she said, "You have white people in there."

I said, "Yes ma'am, I do. They're the Freedom Riders."

She said, "I'm going to tell you, I don't want them in my house." That's when I discovered her militancy. She said, "I cannot go in their homes, and I don't want them in my home. I can't go through the front door of anything that they own and I don't want them coming through my front door. Now you be just as ladylike as you can and serve them lemonade and cookies, and I want them out of the house."

Somehow that weighed on me. I said to myself, Well, she has a point. Then I turned around and I said, "Aunt Chick, these aren't the white people like that. This is a different kind of white group."

James Roberson as a baby

All photographs, unless otherwise noted,
were provided by the individuals pictured.

Pat Shuttlesworth

Fred Shuttlesworth, Jr.

Ricky Shuttlesworth

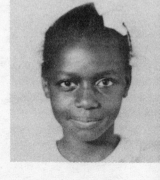

Roy DeBerry
(High school graduation)

Claudette Colvin

Audrey Faye Hendricks

Joseph Lacey

Gwendolyn Patton

Towanner Hinkle

Mary Gadson and
Larry Russell

*Ben, Sr., Ben, Jr., and Fannie Lee Chaney at a memorial service
for James Chaney, August 7, 1964*   Black Star, © Vernon Merritt

Gladis Williams
Courtesy Jim Peppler

Arlam Carr
Courtesy Jim Peppler

Princella Howard   *Courtesy Jim Peppler*

Thelma Eubanks (center)

Frances Foster

Barbara Howard with Stokely Carmichael

Courtesy of Jim Peppler

Euvester Simpson

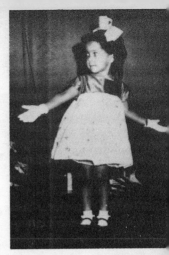

Jawana Jackson

Larry Martin (far left)

Sheyann Webb   *Courtesy Jim Peppler*

A police dog bites the pants leg of a demonstrator in Birmingham, Alabama.

5. *The Children's Crusade*

In April and May 1963, thousands of civil rights demonstrators in Birmingham, Alabama, were attacked by police officers under orders from Police Commissioner Eugene "Bull" Connor. The police wielded nightsticks and unleashed dogs on the marchers. Fire fighters knocked down demonstrators with high-powered water hoses. Many children and adults were injured. Young blacks were jailed by the thousands, while the rest of America and the world watched in horror. So many young people were arrested that these events became known as the Children's Crusade.

The effect of the demonstrations was so great that Birmingham's white business leaders were forced to discuss a timetable for ending segregation in downtown stores and for setting up a plan to hire black sales and office workers.

At a mass meeting on May 6, 1963, Dr. King spoke about the events in Birmingham: "There are those who write history," and "there are those who make history. . . . I don't know how many historians we have in Birmingham tonight. . . . But you are certainly making history. . . . And you will make it possible for the historians of the future to write a marvelous chapter."

AUDREY FAYE HENDRICKS

There was no way for me not to know about the movement. My church, New Pilgrim, was very active. My pastor was secretary of the Alabama Christian Movement for Human Rights, and my mother was the assistant secretary. Whenever anything went on, we were there. When there was news of bombs, we would all go, my mother, my father, my little baby sister, and me. No matter what time of night, we were always a part of it.

I think my very first recollection of what was going on was at a church meeting. I was about seven. They were going to have a small demonstration. I remember leaving the church and walking out to watch the first demonstrators. There was an elderly black man watching, and a dog attacked him. I was in shock. I just couldn't believe that the police would turn the dog loose on an old man.

I remember it being warm the morning I marched. The night before at a meeting, they told us we'd be arrested. I went home and told my mother that I wanted to go. She just said, "Okay." I was in third grade. My teacher knew that I was going, and she cried. She thought, I guess, it was admirable that I would go. Teachers had the threat of losing their jobs.

I did not go to school the day that I went on the march. I wasn't nervous or scared. We started from Sixteenth Street Church. We always sang when we left the church. The singing was like a jubilance. It was a release. And it also gave you calmness and reassurance.

We went down a little side street by Kelly Ingram Park and marched about half a block. Then the police put us in paddy wagons, and we went to Juvenile Hall. There were lots of kids, but I think I may have been the youngest child in there. I was nine. My girlfriend was a year older than me.

Later on they took me to a room where there were some men who asked me questions about the mass meetings. I was nervous when they first called me in. I didn't know what they were going to do to me. The worst thing I thought was that they might kill me. After they started asking me questions, I calmed down a little and thought maybe they're not going to do anything. But it crossed my mind. It was a room of five or six men. All white. And I was little.

I got the impression that they were trying to find out if there were some communistic kinds of things going on. They asked me if they forced us to march, and what was said in the meetings. I told them pretty much what they were doing. That there would be singing and talking about freedom, that kind of thing. They said nothing. I was in there about fifteen minutes. After that they let me go back.

I was in jail seven days. We slept in little rooms with bunk beds. There were about twelve of us in a room. I was in a room with my friends. We called ourselves Freedom Fighters, Freedom Riders. There were only one or two kids in jail who were delinquents. Everybody else was there because of the movement. We ate in a cafeteria. The food wasn't home cooking. I remember some grits, and they weren't too good. My parents could not get word to me for seven days.

We would get some news, like there was no more room in Juvenile Hall. They were taking the rest of the people to the fairgrounds because that was the only place to house them now. The jails were all full. I felt like I was helping to gain what we were trying to get, and that was freedom.

At the end of seven days, they told me my parents were there to get me. I was real glad. They were just smiling and hugging me. I knew they had been nervous 'cause I heard them on the phone talking to friends and saying, "Oh, I'm glad she's back!" I could tell they were proud of me.

JUDY TARVER

I didn't know when I left home for school that day that I was going to participate. Some people weren't going, and some were trying to decide. I was ready to go. We felt in sympathy with all the students in Birmingham. They were just filling up the jails. We hadn't taken our place in the movement yet, and we felt that we should get involved.

We left school after lunch. We joined up with Miles College students, but most of the group was high school kids. When we started out, we didn't think we might be arrested. I thought we would get to the shopping center and be able to parade and demonstrate.

I guess the principal called the Fairfield police, who in turn called the Birmingham police. We were out on this divided highway with grass down the center. We probably didn't walk more than a mile past Miles College before we were arrested. We were walking on the side of the road when the police cars came behind us. They told us to stop, but we just kept walking. We were singing "We Shall Overcome." We started running because it looked like they were going to run us down. They came on the grass with their cars and chased us. Then they went to get school buses, and they hauled us to the jail in Birmingham.

I never went inside that jail. Those who were eighteen had to go in and be fingerprinted. I was seventeen. Reverend King came by and he talked with us outside the fence. We felt better after that. We stood outdoors maybe two to three hours. Then they took us to juvenile detention by bus. By then it started to rain. We stood in the rain for a long time. I was in my white dress. Every senior girl started wearing white dresses the first of May, and wore them for a month until graduation. So there we were in our muddy white dresses.

Finally we got inside. This must have been about eight or nine o'clock at night. We had left school at around one o'clock. They had prepared some peanut butter sandwiches and milk. This was the first thing we had eaten since noon.

The jails were full, so they loaded us on the bus again and took us to Fair Park. This was the same fairgrounds amusement park I couldn't go to as a kid because they didn't allow black people in there. It was pretty ironic.

They took us to the top floor of a two-story barracks building, which was nothing but a large empty room with mattresses on the floor. They had some policewomen assigned to the girls. They searched everybody, and then told us to fall in.

There were no sheets on the mattresses. Some of the people were turning up their noses. The policewomen said, "This is no picnic. This is no pajama party." We hadn't thought about what we were going to be facing.

They turned out the lights, and we went to sleep. That whole room was full. The boys must have been downstairs. I was fortunate. I was there just one night. It was a Friday when we left school, and that Saturday we were let out about twelve or one o'clock.

I was glad to get out. My parents didn't know when I left home that Friday that I was going to participate. Once we were arrested, we couldn't call our families. One of my friends called, I think, so they knew. When I got out, they said that they didn't want to tell me to go, but they were glad that I went. They were proud of me.

We went to school the next week. Some of the boys that were eighteen stayed in jail for a week. In classes we didn't have any difficulties. The teachers didn't criticize any of us for going. The kids that didn't go, I think, felt ashamed that they hadn't.

Our class celebrated our twenty-fifth class reunion in 1988. Our class motto was "No gains without pains." At the reunion we were saying that we were the class that went to jail.

BERNITA ROBERSON

It was Easter, and nobody went shopping. We wouldn't spend money with the white man. That's how we could get to him. He owned all the businesses. So we had no new Easter clothes for two or three Easters. In fact, if you went to church on Easter Sunday and had on something new, you looked out of place.

I don't remember when the mass meetings started, but I think my father was one of the first who was a part of it in Reverend Shuttlesworth's church. You would hear about everything that was going on, and you soon get it in your mind that you want to be a part of it. So every Monday night I went with my father.

I have two brothers. My father had talked with all three of us, particularly me, and said that he did not want us to march. Generally I was a good child. I usually didn't disobey. It was the Thursday before Good Friday, and my mother and father and I were in church. Dr. King made the call for people to join him, and all these people said they'd go to jail with him. You had other people who had been to jail telling their experiences. A friend of mine said, "Let's go!" I felt like a spirit was telling me to get out there. So I went down and volunteered and said that the next morning I would be a part of it.

As you walked down, people clapped, and you got

the sense that all these people were behind you. So many had been before. It was like rotating. Now it's your turn, and you have to go. My father was an usher. When he saw me get up and go, I think he felt okay. My mother was upset. She thought I was a bit young. I was fourteen and very small. She had all the people in the church praying for me that I wouldn't get hurt.

I woke up in the morning, and my family had family prayer with me. We started out from Sixteenth Street Church. We held hands and just walked. Dr. King was leading. Most people were older than me. My father stood on the sidelines.

The police stopped us about a block from the church. They gave us a chance to disperse, but I knew what I was going to have to do. When they put us under arrest, we stepped up into the paddy wagons. I looked back at my daddy. He kind of smiled in support because he knew that somebody from the family was going. And it was the baby child.

They carried us to the county jail. All of us were in the same cell. There may have been about fifty people. Then they started taking out the younger ones to move us to Juvenile. As we went out, Martin King was at the door of the cell because he was in jail also. He hugged us and shook all of our hands as we passed him.

I was not afraid. I felt good that I could make a difference. I was determined to make a difference. I did not want to be intimidated by whites.

I was in jail four days.

In my family growing up, James, my older brother, got involved. My other brother was not that involved. I have real serious beliefs, and I'm more opinionated than the others. I guess I got it from my dad, who saw oppression. He was so angry about it that he would never ride the buses. He could never participate in any of this because his anger was so violent. He didn't do it, so I did it for him.

LARRY RUSSELL

When I got involved in the demonstrations in 1963, I was in high school. My parents supported my decision to get involved, but they were not involved.

I went to a lot of mass meetings. We didn't have transportation, so we walked to them. We knew about them from two radio disc jockeys, Shelley Stewart and Paul White. Paul White used to call the meetings "a party." On the broadcast he'd say, "There's going to be a party Monday night at six at Sixteenth Street Baptist Church, and everybody's invited." We good old Baptists knew there wasn't going to be any dance.

With Shelley back then there was no telling what he'd say. You knew it was coded for the protection of their jobs. The morning *after* a meeting he'd get on the broadcast and he'd say, "Last night there was a mass meeting over at Sixteenth Street Baptist Church, and it appears there were sixteen hundred people there." Then it's news, and he's covered himself. He might add something in a real quick and sly way—"I wonder how many are going to be there Wednesday night?" and then he'd go into a rap.

I was sixteen in 1963, and I expected to be arrested. I wanted to be arrested. I went to jail June 9, 1963. I won't forget it.

Jail was a totally different experience. I'd never been on the other side of the big wall before. They took us in to be fingerprinted. Once the gate closed, we were treated like common criminals. We weren't treated like kids. They didn't want the jails filled. They wanted to make it uncomfortable for us, so we'd call our parents to come and bail us out.

But our intent was not to be bailed out. Matter of fact, with the one phone call they gave me, the first thing I did was to call my mother. "Don't worry about me," I told her. "I'll be okay. We've been arrested and I'm in the city jail. I'm doing fine. There are a bunch of us here. Whatever you do, don't come and get me out."

She was concerned. She sounded tearful on the other end. I said, "Please, this is what I want to do." She said, "Okay."

I was in for ten days.

MARY GADSON

I was not what you call a hero. I was very quiet, and I was really surprised that I was taking part in this. But I think the arrest of my sister Claudette [Chapter Two] had a lot to do with it. I felt a sense of doing right. I thought one day I want to have kids, and I don't want them to go through what I did.

During those days, our parents were basically afraid. I think they would have kept us from doing a lot of things, if they had known about it. My mother didn't know I was going to Sixteenth Street Church. She thought I was going to school, but then I'd shoot a hookey from school to go to Sixteenth Street. She worked for the white folks. They were constantly asking parents, "Is your child involved in this stuff? I hope she isn't." So we couldn't tell.

I'd get to school and then go over the fence. We had listened to Shelley on the radio that morning, so we knew what time to meet. Sometimes if the meeting was at ten o'clock, we would go to our first classes, and then be out for the rest of the day.

I had just a few friends who didn't participate. They were kind of envious. But you have to remember, the majority of the boys who did not participate had parents who were professionals. There were very few of them. Samuel Ullman High School had over twelve hundred kids at that time, and eleven hundred of us were over the fence. We were gone!

At the meetings, we did a lot of singing and talking. "Ain't Gonna Let Nobody Turn Me 'Round" was like an incentive. We also sang a lot of the old spirituals like "Go Down, Moses." We considered Birmingham was Egypt.

One demonstration I remember well. We were in a group that was supposed to march downtown, but we never made it because the police stopped us. Bull Connor was right out here on Sixth Avenue. He had the dogs out there, and he said if we marched, he was going to turn the dogs on us. They had the fire hoses also. That water was strong. It could knock you down. And he let 'em go and sprayed us. I got wet, and I almost got bitten. There were hundreds of us.

They caught a lot of kids, but I wasn't arrested that day. I escaped. I got home out of breath, scared. My parents didn't know I was on that march. I went in and told my mama that we had to run from Bull Connor, and everybody was in jail except me. She told my daddy. He just sat there and shook his head.

I thought Bull Connor was just like his name. He was a bigot, a racist. He had so much hatred in his heart. In fact, I didn't think the man had a heart. I couldn't understand how anybody could hate that much. Just for the color of your skin. I really thought he would burn in hell. Every time I would think about Bull Connor, I always saw fire around him. "Keep the niggers down!" Even with that, for some reason we were not afraid of him. We looked at him like he was an old man who was just about over the hill. Being teenagers, you're not scared of anything.

Myrna Carter

I can't explain why I started getting involved. It was like something drawing me from the inside. I was always the one for the underdog, and problems that affected other people affected me.

And I had a complex. I was tall. I was five feet eight inches when I was twelve. The children would tease me. I began to withdraw, and I would lose myself in books and other things.

One day my friend Carol and I decided to go to one of the meetings. Dr. King spoke, and immediately after we had commitment period. He would tell you to come forward if you were willing to fight for what was right. But you had to take an oath. You had to agree to be nonviolent. You had to agree that if anything would happen, you would turn the other cheek. He said, "If you can't do it, don't come."

People were springing up and going down front like mad. It was just sending chills down me. The next night we went to the meeting and I looked at Carol and she looked at me. She was waiting on me and I was waiting on her. Finally we both got up and went down. They asked us to come the next morning for instructions.

At first I thought I was going to be afraid, but somehow the fear went. The drawing power in Dr. King's voice was like that of no one else who was connected with the struggle. It wasn't that we worshiped him. We certainly did not. He wasn't like that at all. I think that's why he had that power that could make you actually leap and you didn't realize you were leaping.

The very first time I was arrested, we were leaving Sixteenth Street Church trying to make it downtown. They separated us into groups. At first we didn't know why. Reverend Young lined one group up and gave them all signs and a route to go. You could hear the police motorcycles and the paddy wagons out there waiting on us.

This first group came out of the church quietly chanting, "O freedom, O freedom, O freedom over me, and before I be a slave I'll be buried in my grave, and go home to my Lord and be free." They went down Sixteenth Street and immediately WHRRRR, you could hear the motorcycles rev up and start out after them. Then the police arrested them.

While they were busy doing that, the leaders gave us signs and told us to go out Sixth Avenue in the opposite direction. The police thought the first group was all there was going to be that day. So my group got downtown to Newberry's. It was the first time we got all the way there. When the police realized what had happened, someone called the paddy wagon. They lined us up and snatched our signs from us.

There was one well-dressed old white lady who walked up to me. She said, "Why don't you niggers go back to the North. The niggers here is satisfied." I will never forget that. She didn't know who we were. You know, they called it "northern interference." They didn't have sense enough to know that we were not from the North. We were from right here. They thought we didn't have enough guts to do that, so it had to be someone from the North. She didn't touch me or spit on me. She just made that statement and walked off.

Then they hauled us off to jail. In jail we would have prayer meeting in the mornings and at twelve and at night. Prayers from your heart, and freedom songs and Negro hymns. One night when we were in jail, they bombed the Gaston Motel. We were singing before the explosion. We heard the noise and knew something was bombed, but we didn't know what. The police got on the P.A. system and started singing "I Wish I Was in Dixie" over and over. But we didn't lose a beat. We just continued to sing our songs.

At the mass meetings people would say, "I can't go to jail, but here's a couple of dollars. Get yourself something to eat." Or they'd bake a cake and bring it down to the church. If you had gone to jail you were somebody. People would always come up to you and say, "I wish I was you, but I can't." We felt real good about it. I think that's what helped with a lot of the fear, people supporting you. They'd talk to you as if it were an honor to talk to someone who'd gone to jail.

I remember one march very well. We met at New Pilgrim Church that Sunday. Immediately after the service we lined up in two's to march to Memorial Park, directly across from the City Police Department. This particular Sunday we had children and people of all ages. When we got to Memorial Park, Bull Connor was there. The Birmingham fire department was all ready with their hoses. That hose was so long, they had a line of firemen holding it every so many feet. And the policemen were there with their dogs. The dogs were on leashes. They'd lunge, and the police would pull them back. They thought it was funny to let them almost get to us. We were afraid of the dogs, but we were not to show fear. We were to keep walking and singing as if they were not there.

When we got to Memorial Park, Reverend Billups was standing in front of the group, and he said, "We are ready for your fire hoses, your dogs, and anything else!" And tears just started running down his face. I'll never forget it. Bull Connor told the firemen, "Turn the water on! Turn the water on!" But they stood there frozen. "Turn the water on! Turn the water on!" Then he started using profanity, cursing them, shaking the hose and shaking them. "Turn the hose on! Turn it on!" But those people just stood there. They would not turn the hoses on that Sunday. Then the whole group started singing Negro spirituals. It was just something in the air.

THE AFTERMATH: The March on Washington and the Sunday School Bombing

In May 1963, the children had marched, been arrested, and spent time in jail. There was a feeling of triumph, of having acted on your beliefs, of having been a part of change.

The powerful momentum of the civil rights movement coming out of the Birmingham events reached a high point on August 28 of that year. From all over the country a quarter of a million people of all races, religions, and national backgrounds marched on Washington, D.C., in a protest demonstration to end discrimination against blacks. More than two thousand buses, thirty special trains, and thousands of automobiles poured into the capital. It was a sunny day, and people walked the demonstration route from the Washington Monument to the Lincoln Memorial with a sense of enjoyment as well as excitement.

The March on Washington had been planned by A. Philip Randolph, head of the Brotherhood of Sleeping Car Porters, and Bayard Rustin, longtime civil rights activist. All the major civil rights groups helped coordinate the event, and all of the groups' leaders spoke. Dr. Martin Luther King gave his famous "I Have a Dream" speech, in which he told of his vision that "my four little children will one day live in a nation where they will not be judged by the color of their skin, but by the content of their character." That was in August.

In September, there was tragedy. At a Sunday service at Sixteenth Street Baptist Church in Birmingham, a bomb exploded, killing four young black girls, Addie Mae Collins, Denise McNair, Cynthia Wesley, and Carole Robertson. The evil of racism was clear to the world. It could not be hidden behind a sentimental notion of a "southern way of life."

The horror of the bombing affected all decent people, white as well as black. Charles Morgan, a white lawyer, gave a speech in Birmingham the day after the bombing. He asked, "Who did it? . . . We all did it . . . every person in this community who has in any way contributed . . . to the popularity of hatred is at least as guilty . . . as the demented fool who threw that bomb."

Young people were deeply moved by the event.

Audrey Faye Hendricks, Mary Gadson, and Bernita Roberson knew several of the girls who were killed.

AUDREY FAYE HENDRICKS

I was at church at the time, and they came and told my pastor. He let us know that there had been a bombing at Sixteenth Street Baptist Church. People were real upset. They cried. I cried. Later on that night I learned that the girls had died. I wondered how could somebody be so hate-filled about color. I remember seeing Denise's mother at school one day after they had buried her. I don't think she ever taught again. Denise was an only child.

MARY GADSON

I went to school with two of the girls who were killed at the Sixteenth Street bombing. Cynthia Wesley and I sang in the Ullman High School choir together. Denise McNair was at Center Street school with me, although she was younger than I was. Her mother taught me at that school.

I was at home getting ready to go to church when I heard the news on the radio. My whole family was at home. The lady next door called my mama to ask her to turn on the TV. She did, and they had the news report about it. My mama was crying. We all started crying. It was just like family. They told us that as far as they could tell there were some deaths; but at that time they didn't know how many. Then the report came later that it was four girls that had been killed.

It was truly shocking. One of my girlfriends was in the same Sunday school class that morning with the girls. When the bomb went off, the head of one of the girls passed straight in front of her. My girlfriend had to go for psychiatric help. She didn't get hurt physically.

I couldn't believe anybody would do something like that at a church. We knew they had bombed houses and cars. That was nothing new. But when you take it out of the street and into the church, it was like nothing was sacred anymore.

BERNITA ROBERSON

When the bomb went off, we felt it in our Sunday school class four blocks away. I lived across the street from Bethel Baptist [Reverend Shuttlesworth's church], so that I knew the feeling of a bomb. In about fifteen minutes, word got to us that they had bombed Sixteenth Street, where the children were in Sunday school. Then our Sunday school immediately turned out, and everybody got together in prayer.

I was a friend of Denise McNair. I knew her grandfather. He owned a cleaners, and I knew her from there. I was a flower girl for her funeral. Three of the funerals were held at the same time. There was nothing like seeing those three families there, and the three coffins. I was just trying to understand how somebody could do this to children. To this day, I don't really know.

I wasn't angry because you were taught not to be. You were taught to forgive people. Things were happening so fast during that time, you didn't know what to expect next. Anger and sorrow were just a part of trying to get accomplished what you wanted.

In Jackson, Mississippi, whites pour sugar, ketchup and mustard over the heads of restaurant lunch counter sit-in demonstrators in June, 1963.

6. *The Closed Society: Mississippi and Freedom Summer*

Mississippi stood out even among southern states for its brutal enforcement of segregation. Almost half the population of the state was black, and there were more beatings, "disappearances," and lynchings than in any other state in the nation. Mississippi was a "closed society," as many called it.

In 1955 the rest of America woke up one morning to headlines about a singularly brutal killing. Emmett Till, a fourteen-year-old boy from Chicago, had been visiting relatives in Mississippi when he was tortured and murdered for allegedly talking "improperly" to a white woman. In a segregated Mississippi courthouse, two white men were tried for the murder and acquitted. Several months later, they admitted to an Alabama journalist that they had indeed murdered Till.

The tactics of violence in Mississippi were meant not only to punish a particular individual, but to intimidate other blacks. As one of Till's murderers said, "I like niggers in their place. . . . I just decided it was time a few people got put on notice." In 1955 several other Mississippi blacks were also killed. One of the victims was Reverend George Lee. Euvester Simpson was nine years old at the time, and Reverend Lee was her father's friend. "Everything just went crazy at my house when that happened. My father went to the funeral. People knew that Reverend Lee had been active in the NAACP. If they were thinking of doing anything, that put a stop to it. I felt scared."

Until the beginning of the sixties, most civil rights activity in Mississippi had been under the auspices of the NAACP. By 1961, SNCC had its first fieldworker, Bob Moses, in Mississippi. This was the beginning of activism by large groups of young people.

Very few blacks in the state were allowed to vote. Sometimes they were physically intimidated and threatened to prevent them from registering. Often they were kept from registering by blatantly discriminatory rules. Applicants, for example, were required to pass literacy tests and interpret obscure sections of the state constitution. Blacks were almost always told they had failed the tests; whites, on the other hand, even if illiterate, were routinely registered.

Segregationists often tried to excuse the absence of black voters by arguing that black people weren't interested in voting. In 1962 the major civil rights groups, CORE, SNCC, NAACP, and SCLC, formed the Council of Federated Organizations (COFO), which began work on a major voter rights project. Throughout 1963 young people worked all over Mississippi trying to register black voters. They organized a Freedom Party open to anyone, regardless of race, and sponsored a Freedom Vote for governor and lieutenant governor. As a result of that effort, more than eighty thousand black Mississippians voted in the freedom election, giving the lie to the claim that they weren't interested. Kept out of regular Democratic Party politics in the state, civil rights workers then formed the Mississippi Freedom Democratic Party (MFDP), which enrolled thousands of disenfranchised blacks.

One of COFO's most ambitious projects was Freedom Summer, 1964. It was a plan to bring nearly a thousand students, mostly white, to Mississippi to work on a massive voter registration drive and other community projects. The young people set up freedom schools with classes in black history as well as regular school subjects. Meetings were held in churches, empty lots, homes, community centers— wherever space could be found. In the evenings there were training classes for adults for voter registration. The freedom schools had a powerful impact on young people. Thelma Eubanks, for example, went every day in McComb.

We were introduced to black authors who we didn't know anything about at the time. Richard Wright and James Baldwin. I thought they were good. I also remember *Freedom Road* by Howard Fast and *Strange Fruit* by Lillian Smith. We hadn't had any of that at school. All we had was Harriet Tubman and the Underground Railroad, Eli Whitney and the cotton gin, and George Washington Carver and the peanut. I guess it was the first time I really heard black success stories. And the freedom school was the first time I had a social relationship with whites. It just made me know that everybody in the world wasn't like the southerners.

The summer project, so successful in its outreach to Mississippi blacks, actually began in tragedy with the disappearance of three civil rights workers, Michael Schwerner, James Earl Chaney, and Andrew Goodman. In 1963, Michael and Rita Schwerner, a white couple, moved from New York City to Meridian, Mississippi, to open a CORE center. Together with James Chaney, a black Mississippian, they set up programs for the area youth and organized voter registration projects. Their work angered local segregationists, who wanted them out of the county.

At the beginning of the summer of 1964, Schwerner and Chaney went to Ohio to train student volunteers for Freedom Summer. It was there they met Andrew Goodman, a white college student from New York. When the three young men returned to Mississippi, they went to investigate the burning of a black church in Longdale, near the town of Philadelphia. On their return trip to Meridian, they were arrested and later released by Neshoba County police officers. That was June 21. For the next six weeks no one could find a trace of them. Then on August 4, after a tip from an informant, FBI agents found their bullet-riddled bodies buried in an earthen dam a few miles from Philadelphia.

No one was ever tried for their murder. Three years later, eighteen men, many Klan members, were charged in federal court with conspiring to deprive the victims of their civil rights. Among them were Neshoba County Sheriff Lawrence Rainey and Deputy Sheriff Cecil Ray Price. Seven of the men were convicted, including Price. He was sentenced to six years in prison. Rainey was acquitted.

Freedom Summer went on, despite the disappearance and murder of the three young activists. Student workers from the North joined civil rights activists in the South. Together they set up hundreds of freedom schools for young people, worked with thousands of adults preparing for voter registration exams, and forged deep ties with one another. As Euvester Simpson says:

I made friendships with not only other black people, but with white people. I had never had really close friendships with people from other backgrounds. It created a bond between us. I could go right now and find somebody from those days in the movement that I hadn't seen in twenty years, and the bond is there.

LARRY MARTIN

My father died when we were babies. We were five kids and my mama and my grandmother. My mother fixed hair downtown, and my grandmother had a little eating establishment right next door to the beauty parlor. It was called Calmese's Grill.

We lived across the street from the COFO office, right down in the heart of town [Meridian]. We were little kids running around down there, and one day we saw those white guys going up those stairs. They looked different, not like the ones you'd see around here all the time. They'd talk to us and tell us, "You guys, come over and play sometime." So we started going up there. We used to go and just read. First time I ever saw so many books. All kinds.

I was eleven when Mickey Schwerner came. I spent lots of time with Mickey and Rita. They were funny, most always happy. He used to do a lot of magic tricks for us. He'd take Ping-Pong balls in his hands and say, "It's over here," and pull it from somewhere else. It fascinated us. We had never seen that before. Rita and Frankie Wright taught us freedom songs. We used to sing "We Shall Overcome" and "Ain't Gonna Let Nobody Turn Me 'Round." Those were my favorites.

When James Chaney came on the scene, I learned what it was all about. James was a nice, easygoing fella, quiet most of the time. Come around with his hands in his overalls. He wore a blue T-shirt. He was real friendly. He was different from most black guys you'd see. Most guys would be hanging in the pool rooms, or hanging on the corner. But he was up there. He had his job to do. Always seemed to be happy and ready to work.

I was listening to what they were talking about. About how the white man was treating the blacks so bad, couldn't get decent jobs, had to drink out of a certain water fountain, and things like that. And I said to myself, I think that's right to fight against that 'cause a man is a man. I don't have some business about somebody because of what color they are. Ever since I was a little bitty boy, I felt like that.

We'd go to the COFO office every day and stay until night. They never told us to go home. They let us stay and play as long as we wanted to. We'd read and talk and play games. I wanted to be in the demonstrations. I wanted to be a part of it. At the airport, for instance, they wouldn't serve blacks. I remember Mickey, Preston, James Chaney, and, I believe, Ben [James's eleven-year-old brother], we all went out one day to eat. We all ordered apple pie. The lady served us, but she put salt on the pie. We ate it.

We also went uptown to Kress's. They had a certain side for blacks to eat on. Mickey said, "Well, we're going to change that." So we went up there to eat dinner, and we all sat on the white side. They served us. They didn't really want to do it, but they served us. Me and Ben Chaney were the youngest in most everything we did.

I was arrested a couple of times. Once when we were boycotting Kress's, like always, the policemen came and put us all in the paddy wagon. They kept me and Ben, and then let us go. They'd take us to scare us, talk to us real mean, tell us to go on. But the older men, they kept them. We went back to tell

Rita at the COFO office what happened.

At the time, I knew there weren't black people voting, and we needed those votes so we could get people in office that we thought would do a good job. My mama and grandmother got registered when COFO came. They used to have those big rallies and meetings. We went to different churches here, getting people registered to vote.

I remember Mickey saying if we get the vote, we can make a change. That sounded about right to me. We started passing out leaflets saying there was going to be a meeting. We'd walk for miles a day passing out pamphlets, trying to get people registered. We weren't out there shooting basketball or playing marbles. A lot of times I didn't even go swimming. I'd rather pass out leaflets, sit-in, or something. I enjoyed doing what I was doing. I felt it was right.

My mama didn't worry about us when we were at the office 'cause she knew we was with Mickey, and we were in good hands. My grandmother would cook the meals at the restaurant, and they'd come and eat, Mickey and Rita, Frank and Judy Wright. They were the very first whites that ate there. That's where all the people from the COFO office would come. She'd fix them a big dinner free.

Before COFO, I didn't really come in contact with white people at all. School was all black, teachers were all black, principal was black. Stores had white people. We'd buy tennis shoes, or candy, but as far as talking with them, or communicating with them, we didn't do that. They were very mean in those days. They would not give you money in your hand. They'd throw it down. They'd watch you real hard when you were going out, as if you were going to steal something. I didn't like that. I've never been a thief, and it made you feel bad.

The Klan were hateful, rednecks you call them nowadays. Just real coldhearted to black people. They were young guys, middle-aged, and old men. Like the guy that owned this electric company. He was an old man, and he didn't like nobody black. I mean just for nothing. We'd walk by and he'd come out and try and make us get off the sidewalk. "Get off the sidewalk, get in the streets!" he'd yell.

And the people at the laundry right down the street from the COFO office, we saw them loading the sheets up in there one Saturday night. And the laundry wasn't open at night. They had a lot of Klansmen there.

We had some mean policemen. They were so mean, you'd know them by name. We had one who became a judge. He finally got voted out. He tried to change his image, but he didn't change his heart.

When the policemen used to see us just walking together, black and white, they'd stop us for nothing, and take the men to jail. That's what happened with Freeman Corcroft. He was white, and he used to come down every summer just to work with the kids. He'd take us to the black pool over in the East End. They had a white pool, but we couldn't get in that one. He went in the black pool. Nobody tried to stop him there. We weren't like that.

One day he had taken us swimming. We were walking back, and the policeman stopped him because he was white and with us. It was very unusual for a white guy to be leading a group of black kids. The policeman asked him what he was doing with all these children. He said, "These are my friends, and we're just coming back from swimming." They didn't believe him. They thought he was doing something else, but he wasn't. He was just always with us. They took him to jail, and we were really mad. We went up to tell Mickey what happened. They went and got him, paid the fine.

Mickey and the others had told us there was going to be a lot of people coming down for the summer. People were coming from everywhere, black and white, to work with us, give us help and support. We was glad. We needed it. Mississippi, ooh it got really rough down here, especially back in the sixties. Black man didn't hardly stand a chance. I remember about Medgar Evers [field secretary of the NAACP in Mississippi]. He was in the same field of work as Mickey and Chaney, and he'd lost his life in it.

Mickey and them were saying that they had to go to Philadelphia [Mississippi] where the black church had been burned. They were going to check things out and see what was going on. We knew they were going up there early Sunday morning. Andrew Goodman was here just that one day. He got here that Saturday, and they left that Sunday morning. I didn't get to know him good.

Ben and I were the ringleaders of the young guys. They let us go where other kids couldn't go, or didn't want to go, 'cause we weren't scared of anything. At eleven and twelve years old, we weren't afraid. On Saturday Mickey had promised us that we could go with them, but later Saturday night he said, "No, you guys can't go. Something might happen. It just might not work." So Ben and I got mad. Oh, we were angry.

We never saw them alive again.

Ben and I were waiting in the COFO office because they were supposed to have been back. We waited and waited and waited. Still no word. Then someone got in touch with the sheriff up there. The sheriff told them that he had arrested them, and then let them go. I thought they were dead, killed. I believed they were dead 'cause I knew Philadelphia was mean, mean people there, very hateful and prejudiced people. In 1964 they didn't want to see no blacks riding together with no whites. They'd rather see anything than that. That's why Mickey told us we couldn't go.

The policemen and sheriffs were coming up, asking questions. All kinds of men with suits on, asking questions. The office was busy then. People were trying to find out what was going on. You heard so many stories. I think it was my grandmother said she remembered a man come in to eat and said that when it started to rain, he saw three streaks of lightning in the sky. I never will forget that as long as I live. I thought it meant they were dead and buried.

One white man used to bring bread and things to my grandmother's place. One day she said to him, "Sure was awful what they did to those three guys up there, isn't it?" My grandma said he dropped his head and he looked so funny. When they did get the men who killed them, he was in that group. Bringing her bread like that for years. He was a little short man.

After we found out for sure they were dead, it was chaos in the COFO office. There was a lot of crying going on. Everything went wild. Right after that it looked like the whole office just vanished. Like the heart of it was gone. Those guys were the backbone. After they left, everybody else started leaving. Never an office again. I wish somebody would have stayed here, keep that place open. Why did everybody seem like they had to give up because they were gone? There was a leader in the crowd somewhere. Somebody could have carried the torch on after all they'd been through.

I sure missed it. I missed it a lot. It was all of our friends, all of our fun. I miss Mickey and James. And I miss Rita. I miss the work, too, that we did there. It made you feel good. Like you were doing something that really meant something.

When we got older, Ben and I talked on making a new COFO office. I would like to get the same office that Mickey and James used. It brings back so many memories, that building. I'd do what Mickey and them did. We got a man here says he can't find nobody black good enough to stay working for him. I know that's a lie. I would get on his case first. Get him to straighten out, or we're going to boycott his store.

I would work with kids. I'd spent time with them like Mickey and them did with us, soften their hearts up. A lot of times it'll save you from being in trouble later in your life.

I believe if it weren't for Mickey and them now, I don't know what kind of guy I would have been. That's right. They really made a difference when I was growing up. I'm glad that I had the opportunity to meet those guys and to know them and work with them. I loved the work they were doing. I'd really like to be a part of it again.

BEN CHANEY

We used to watch the Freedom Riders on television. In early '63 my brother got involved in the freedom rides. By him talking to me and my family, that's when I got an idea what the movement was about. To be a Freedom Rider meant sitting in the front of the bus. But it didn't only mean riding on a bus. Bucking the system, not getting off the sidewalk when white people walked by, not saying "mister." Anything that would be a sign of rebellion, rebelling against the system, rebelling against the status quo, rebelling against segregation.

My brother was scolded and told not to do that anymore by my father and my mother. The older people were telling him not to get involved, but he continued. I thought about being a Freedom Rider. Whatever my brother wanted to do or did, I wanted to do.

Mickey and Rita [Schwerner] organized the community center in the spring, and I went every day. I was in school at the time, and usually after school I would come by the center. Sometimes my brother would bring me home. I was eleven years old. I played with the typewriter, played Ping-Pong, sang freedom songs. "Keep Your Eyes on the Prize" was my favorite. The one I disliked the most was "We Shall Overcome." It was so slow.

There were no organized activities for black kids in the community, and the Freedom Center offered some. We were kept pretty busy. It was also a learning experience. There was a Freedom School where we received tutoring in English, arithmetic, writing, those things. There was always something happening then. You never got bored.

We would sit around on the floor in a group and everybody would sing. There was always a discussion going on. Mostly adults would talk about voter registration, and what was happening. They talked about the latest attack, who got whupped recently by the racists. And we were listening. It was usual for a black person to get beaten up by southern segregationists. It was unusual for a white person to get beaten up by other whites for being with blacks. But over a period of time, you understand, the whites hated those other whites just as much as they hated the blacks.

We was picketing some five-and-ten stores: Woolworth's, Kress's, and others that wouldn't hire blacks behind the counter. Outside there would be a circle, marching in front of the store. Depending upon how many people you had, the circle might stretch for a whole block. If there were not too many, then it would just be around the entrance of the store. You would march around, carrying your sign and singing freedom songs.

I think the worst demonstration I was on was where this big redneck, this big racist, took my picket sign away and tore it up. Then he grabbed me up in the collar, threw me down, and told me to leave and that he'd better not see me again. I walked around the corner and I was scared. I didn't know what to do. So I went to the COFO office, got another sign, and went back on the demonstration. That's where I got hit in the head. I was bleeding, but it was okay. It was okay to be hit. It was okay to go to jail.

I was arrested more than twenty-one times before I was twelve years old. "Demonstrating without a permit." That was what they locked everybody up for. Because I was a juvenile, only eleven for most of my arrests, I would go to jail, and then they would put me in a holding cell, or they would set me on a bench right outside the courtroom. We would wait until an adult came and got us out.

In a couple of demonstrations, Mickey Schwerner would come and get me out. Most of the time it would be my brother. He was pretty quiet, but I remember waiting one time for him to come and get me. I could hear his steps in the hallway, and he was saying, "I come for my brother." I was glad. He was proud of me. I was glad to be there too. That's where the action was at in the sixties. That was it.

My brother and Mickey and Goodman left on a Sunday morning [to go to Philadelphia, Mississippi]. The next morning I woke up, expecting my brother to be back. They had promised to take me somewhere, and they didn't come back. The minister who lived down the street from my house came up and told my moms that nobody'd heard from them all day. He was going to Philadelphia to look for them. That's how we got the word. Reverend Porter came up and told us.

During the summer, during the disappearance [from June 21 to August 4], I was very much involved. That's when I got arrested quite a few times. Before the summer, I could go off by myself sometimes and do things on my own. But during that summer, I always had to have an adult. My momma said that.

She was more and more nervous about the whole situation. She grew up in an environment where from a very early age she had seen others in her family disappear, and no one knew anything.

I think that my mother believed that my brother and the others were dead. I think she believed that because she's been there longer and that was the way of life with her. I think my sisters believed that they were dead. But I can pretty much say that until the funeral, I didn't think so. I just knew my brother. I knew that he would find a way to come through. He always came through. And I just knew that if there was any way for him to come through, he would be driving up the driveway in the morning. No doubt about it.

> *Ben spoke at a memorial service for his brother. Neshoba County Sheriff Lawrence Rainey and Deputy Sheriff Cecil Ray Price, who were later arrested in the case, were there. Ben's last words were, "And I want us all to stand up here together and say just one thing. I want the sheriff to hear this good. We ain't scared no more of Sheriff Rainey!"*

I had been told a thousand times by people who shaped my whole thinking pattern that they [Rainey and Price] killed my brother. I thought, How can I get back? What can I do to them to hurt them also? At the memorial somebody asked me what I thought, so I just said what I thought at the moment. After I made that speech, my father gave me a hard time. He was talking, "Forget it. Let bygones be bygones." I guess he was saying mercy, or forgiveness, and all that stuff.

What I remember most is how sad the whole affair was. Throughout the funeral and the memorial service, I kept wondering why didn't people do something. Why didn't my father, my grandfather, my great-grandfather? Why wasn't things made different? Why wasn't change taking place then, so that this event wouldn't be taking place now? I felt a desire to do something to hurt the people that hurt my brother. At that time I couldn't do anything. Even now I can't do anything. But now I'm mature enough to realize that there are things in the work I'm now doing with the James Earl Chaney Foundation about voter registration that I think is not for revenge. It's like a continuation of what happened in the sixties.

I didn't have any idea this would be history. Having a sense of black people being put in an American history book was unrealistic. That's the way it was. When my brother and his companions were missing and they were looking for the bodies, they found more than seven additional black people who had died over that period of time who were involved in the movement. They had disappeared. Nobody searched for them. Nobody was concerned about them. Nobody even talks about them now. So it was like another black person gone.

JOHN STEELE

When I was a kid, a young black man was being transported to a mental institution. He was handcuffed by the sheriff and his deputies. En route to the facility, they let him out and shot him behind the head, and nothing was done. I knew then that we were in for a long, long struggle. I thought maybe this place, Neshoba County, might be the only place that was like this. Maybe one day it would change.

I used to look at television a lot. Out of the super heroes—Roy Rogers, the Lone Ranger, Superman, Batman—that stood for right and justice, I couldn't understand why they couldn't come here and do the same things. Straighten up Neshoba County.

The first time that I met Michael Schwerner and James Chaney was at our home [in Longdale, Mississippi]. I was ten years old. They was telling us about so much wrong, and our rights. Michael Schwerner was always talking about the constitution and what wasn't right. It was enlightening. Really educated me into knowing that there were rights on written documents, and from 1865 we were free.

Once after a rally Schwerner said, "We have come here to die if necessary." And that puzzled me. I looked at him and said this man is talking about dying, and I'm just now getting to know him, and I like him, too. After the services I asked him, "Why you want to talk about dying?" He said, "One day, young Mr. Steele, you might find something worth dying for. Freedom is worth dying for, fighting for other people's freedom."

At the end of May 1964, there was a meeting at Mount Zion Church in Longdale to talk about setting up a voter registration project. Michael Schwerner and James Chaney spoke. Less than three weeks after the organizing meeting, Mount Zion Church was burned to the ground by a white mob.

I remember that night very vividly. We started off in the truck to go to an official board meeting of the church, my sister, my mama, me, and my daddy. Mr. Jim Cole had walked past going down the road, and we picked him up. When we got to the church, me and my sister stayed outside under the night light.

We were playing with this frog when a car came by and stopped right out in front of the church. We saw a white fella get out and look up at the church. I was curious why he was looking up there. We went in, and I ran over to my father and I said, "Hey, there's somebody out there looking at us." They carried on with some more church business. Finally we sang the dismissal song, and they said a prayer.

It was my job to cut off the lights in the church. I was standing on top of the bench over the light switch, waiting for them to turn on the headlights of the cars. I looked over in the corner, and I saw the back door of the church was open. It was on the same side as the cemetery. I flicked the lights off in a big hurry, and I saw something white, and I know that door opened. I took me a good look, and CLAP, I ran out and jumped up on the truck and said, "Daddy, somebody's in the church!" It seemed right then that it was a nightmare.

There was a car sitting in the driveway with three or four white males inside. Mr. Jim Cole got on the back of the truck. My sister was closest to my mother, and I was beside my dad. My mother pushed my sister down as we were going into the road. I popped up to look. As we got to the road, the cars came up and blocked us in. I was peeping, and the guy told my father to cut off the lights. I looked out the back windshield and I could see the other people leaving. Then they asked my father, "Where are those boys?" Mr. Jim Cole said he'd do the talking because my father had a temper.

I instantly knew who he was talking about, Schwerner and Chaney. Mr. Jim said, "What boys you talking about?"

The white man said, "You know damn well what boys I'm talking about. If you all leave them alone, we'll help you all." Meaning we should stay away from the civil rights people.

I didn't know who that white man was, but some of the cars were very familiar. There was a pickup truck, and there were only two in this area. There was a white '63 Ford Galaxy, and there wasn't but two of those in this area. One of the guys had a limp, and I didn't know but one guy who had a limp like that.

Then we heard a shot on the other end, and they let us go on home. But during that time we didn't sleep in the bed. We slept under the bed. The very next day. Mr. Bud Cole came over, and we learned about the church burning down. He was beaten so badly, they wanted to take him to the hospital.

Later on that day we went on over to the church. It was in rubble. I had a fear for Michael Schwerner and James Chaney. And also for myself, and more for my father. About spring of 1964 it had gotten dangerous for my family. We received threats in the mail. My father was harassed. They threatened his life and threatened to burn his house. Later on some of them even said he should have died when Michael Schwerner, Jim Chaney, and Andrew Goodman did.

My father didn't want Schwerner and Chaney to come back because of the danger. When they drove up, it was just like a bad dream. They came to the house that Sunday about two P.M. It was after dinner. My father told them that they shouldn't have come. He said, "It's too dangerous. You need to spend the night. Either that, or let me and my brothers ride with you, and we'll get our guns."

Michael Schwerner said no to the guns 'cause the movement wasn't about violence of any type. He also couldn't spend the night because he said he had to be back in Meridian. They were having a meeting that evening. I remember even the way they were dressed, where they sat at the table.

The next morning, Monday morning, we were getting ready for breakfast, and the radio station asked anybody who knew the whereabouts of Michael Schwerner, James Chaney, Andrew Goodman to get in touch with the COFO office in Meridian. I knew and everybody else in the house knew that something real bad had happened to them. The possibility of them being dead was actual fact.

Everything went into a turmoil. My cousins, my uncles, and different people from other black neighborhoods were all in the bushes. They were armed and ready. My uncle and cousins, they don't believe in just giving your life. They believed in protecting themselves. Cars were coming by. Mailboxes and crosses were being burned. The kids were under the beds.

I remember when the FBI came. I remember this inspector taking me to the church and talking to me. I was telling him he had to find these people who had done this. He said, "Why do you think they did it?" I said, "They threatened to kill my father, so I know they killed them."

People were just combing the woods looking for the bodies—the Navy, the National Guard, aircraft flying over, helicopters landing and picking back up again. There was no way you could turn around anywhere.

Just before they found those bodies, it rained, lightning, electrical storms for weeks and weeks, night and day. My mama said, "It's the Lord. That's those boys' blood crying." And shortly after that, they were found.

EUVESTER SIMPSON

When I was born, my parents were sharecroppers. We moved to Itta Bena when I was eight or nine years old. My parents owned a small grocery store there.

Itta Bena was almost literally divided by the railroad track. My neighborhood, of course, was not mixed. It was an all-black community, and I went to an all-black school. In my neighborhood everybody was poor, really poor.

I left Itta Bena when I was about thirteen and went to live with an older sister in Wisconsin. I came back to Mississippi the last semester of my senior year in high school. It was the winter of 1963, and I was seventeen.

When I got back, I saw all this activity going on. A friend of mine invited me to come to a mass meeting with her. I was absolutely amazed that there were these young black men and women, not much older than I, who were talking about civil rights and the right to vote. They were saying they needed everybody to get involved.

I connected immediately. I knew that was what I needed to do right then. My parents didn't give me a lot of support, but they didn't really try too hard to discourage me.

There were mass meetings at the area churches in Itta Bena and Greenwood. And there were lots of young people walking the streets from house to house, canvassing, trying to get people to understand how important it was to vote. They were saying that if we organized and we acted as a group, then maybe we could change some things. I didn't like the way things were. I didn't like living in an inadequate house. I didn't like not having money to buy clothes. So I became a full-time SNCC worker. When I got out of high school that June [1963], I moved to Greenwood and I started working out of the SNCC office. I remember the salary well. After taxes, $9.64 a week.

The main objective was voter registration, so that's

what I did. First, I would introduce myself. I would tell them that I was from Itta Bena to let them know that I was not from out-of-state. Nobody could claim that we were "outside agitators," as they liked to call us. Then I would tell them, "I'm scared too, but I think that this is something that's important enough to risk even going to jail."

During that summer of 1963 I met Mrs. Fannie Lou Hamer. She lived in Ruleville, not that far from Greenwood, and she was very active. She would often come over to the SNCC office and attend mass meetings. We got to be really good friends. She'd always ask me if I'd called my mother lately, or when was the last time I'd been home.

When you heard Martin Luther King speak, you had to stop what you were doing and listen. It was the same way with her. She was that powerful. She did not have much formal education, but she was willing to be a spokesperson. It didn't bother her if she spoke to the president, or to the Senate, or whatever. She was a very caring and giving person. I don't know why certain people are chosen to do certain things. She always said that she wasn't anything special, that it was God working through her to do whatever it was to be done.

In 1963 Euvester was arrested and imprisoned with Fannie Lou Hamer and a group of civil rights workers in Winona, Mississippi. The whole country learned of this event when later, in a television interview during the Democratic Party Convention in Atlantic City, Mrs. Hamer described how she was beaten.

* * *

I went with Mrs. Hamer to South Carolina to a citizenship school. They taught you how to go out into your community and organize. Eight or ten of us went on a bus from Greenwood.

We stayed in South Carolina about a week. On the way back, every time there was a rest stop, we would get off to use the white side of the bus terminal. We knew what we were doing. Nothing had happened on the way down, and on the way back, we did the same thing. At Columbus, Mississippi, we used the white side of the bus station. The next stop was in Winona, and I think they must have been warned because the patrolmen were there waiting for us. They would not let us into the white side of the bus station.

As we were leaving, Annell Ponder, who was in our group, got out a pad and pencil. I was standing there with her, and she took down the license number of the patrol car that was parked out front. That's when they threw seven of us into a car and took us to jail.

They questioned us all night. After they had talked to us as a group, they put us two people per cell. I shared a cell with Mrs. Hamer. Then they took us out one at a time. I looked very young. I was seventeen, but I looked like I was about fourteen or fifteen years old. They really beat Annell Ponder very badly. They were trying to force her to say "Yessir" to them, and she never would. There was another young girl with us, June Johnson, who was about fifteen, but June was very tall for her age, and she was badly beaten. Then they got around to Mrs. Hamer. There were two black trustees. The police gave them whiskey and got them drunk and made them do the beating.

When they got to me, they took me into this cell with the two trustees. They made me lie facedown on a cot, and they were just about to start beating on me when the jailer came in and said, "Don't hit her!" By that time the bus we had been on had made it back to Greenwood. I guess phone calls were coming in from all over, wondering what they were doing with us. So then they were afraid to do any more.

I remember sitting up the rest of the night with Mrs. Hamer. She had put her hands back to try to keep some of the straps from hitting her head. And so her hands were all black-and-blue and swollen. She got really sick during the night and developed a fever. I put cold towels on her forehead, trying to get the fever down. She was really sick, and we were all so upset. Nobody got any sleep. So you know what we did? We sang freedom songs all through the night.

We were in jail about four days.

I remember after that, I really wasn't frightened. I was just more determined than ever that some changes had to be made. I know I never thought once that we were going down in history books, or making history. I just knew that I could do my little bit.

I think being involved was probably the most important thing I've ever done in my whole life. It taught me first of all that black people could come together, and we could organize, and we could make some things happen for ourselves and for other people as well. I knew that was where I was supposed to be, and it was just so right. I wouldn't trade it for anything in the world, even though we lost some people along the way. We risked our own lives, but we made it through, and we did make a difference.

There's a lot more that needs to be done, and I would like for my children to get involved. When I tell them about some of the things I went through, they cannot conceive of it. I could not walk into a McDonald's, something as simple as that, and order a burger. That's the way things were. And they weren't that way because that's just the way they were. They were deliberately planned that way.

Roy DeBerry

I think I understood very early that one way to make change was by getting people registered to vote. So in 1963, when I was in high school, I spent time canvassing in Holly Springs with a fellow named Michael.

We went to the homes of teachers when we were canvassing. We found they were oftentimes the reluctant ones because they knew that if they took the risk, the local school board would fire them. The teachers were also concerned about my getting involved with these "outside troublemakers" coming in to upset the status quo.

To some extent I was very sensitive to that point. I understood that others shouldn't come in and say, "I have all the answers." We should work together to do what we have to do. It was about local people themselves doing for themselves.

In my town and a lot of Mississippi towns, black people and white people did not socially interact. Yet we were interacting with SNCC workers, and of course the SNCC workers were interacting with other local people. While I didn't have any problem going to a café, or riding in a car with a white person, I was conscious of what I was doing. I knew it was not safe, but I knew it was something that had to be done.

I think that I was afraid a lot of times. What's amazing is that when you are afraid, you can deal with your fear if you don't allow it to cripple you. You deal with it by keeping doing things. Once you commit yourself to something, even as a child, and you think it's right, then it's much easier to deal with the fear.

Mississippi was probably one of the toughest states in the South at that point. I think it was different from Alabama and Georgia and Louisiana. There's no question there are some tough spots in southwest Georgia and all over the country, of course. But the bottom line was that Mississippi was toughest, at least from 1955 and the Emmett Till murder on.

We knew about blacks disappearing and being murdered. We heard about the shooting of Medgar Evers in June of '63. I knew he was the NAACP field secretary. At that point he was probably the major leader in Mississippi. I was shocked, but again that told us what the potential was for violence, and how you had to be ready for psychopaths when you took the system on.

As the news first came through that three civil rights workers had disappeared, I think everybody who had been a part of the movement knew that when you disappear in Mississippi, you're dead. The thing that shocked me was that they were crazy enough to kill two white people. Now that sounds strange, but even at that age we knew that black people were being killed all the time. And with the national press on the scene, we didn't quite understand why they had taken the risk to kill two whites.

A few weeks after the bodies of the three civil rights workers were found, the Democratic Party

*Convention opened in Atlantic City, New Jersey.
President Johnson was nominated for reelection.
The Mississippi Freedom Democratic Party sent
a delegation headed by Fannie Lou Hamer and
Aaron Henry to show America that blacks in
Mississippi weren't allowed to participate in reg-
ular state Democratic Party politics. Roy went to
the convention with other SNCC workers.*

I was seventeen. I had been in Memphis a number of
times and to St. Louis, but I had never been north. I
was excited about being there. It was an election year,
so it was a big period.

I heard Fannie Lou Hamer in Atlantic City, and
earlier in Greenwood at a church meeting. One of her
favorite expressions was, "I'm sick and tired of being
sick and tired!" She was talking about the need for
people to stand up and have courage, register to vote.
She was a powerful speaker, a woman who came from
the soil. She was not trained in terms of education,
but just wise and courageous. Oh, a powerful woman!
I felt proud particularly because she came out of Mississippi and out of the Delta.

The regular Democratic Party in Mississippi was
lily white, and everybody knew that. Black folk had
not been allowed to vote except for the mock election
we had had. Going to the convention was an attempt
to put the nation on the spot. At the very least, we
could ask Johnson to do what we thought was right,
which was to unseat the regular Mississippi Democratic delegation and to seat the MFDP.

I don't think we felt that was actually going to happen, but just going through the process itself was
good. It would give us an opportunity to participate
in the political process at a level that we had not par-

ticipated in before, at least in recent times.

All these civil rights workers were there, all around the boardwalk just interacting with people. We couldn't get inside because we didn't have tickets. So we camped out on the boardwalk. There were speeches going on all the time. I remember Stokely Carmichael giving a speech out there. It was almost like a pep rally to keep the spirit up, to keep people's eyes on the prize.

The Credentials Committee at the Democratic Convention refused to seat the MFDP instead of the all-white state Democratic Party. The committee proposed a compromise plan that MFDP rejected.

I was hearing those political sophisticates saying, "Let's take something, because something is better than nothing." And I heard Fannie Lou Hamer saying, "Let's not do this." I was so proud of the stance that Mrs. Hamer took. I think she was just right on target, and I was very proud that she was unwilling to compromise. While I understood that there were forces saying this was politically naive, from the standpoint of pride and the movement and the people, I thought she was absolutely correct. So I didn't think it was a sad moment at all, not for me personally.

The movement shaped me in a way that I wouldn't have been shaped otherwise. I look at some of my classmates that went through school the same time I did. While some of them may have made it materially and have "good jobs," making fairly decent salaries or in their own business, I get a sense, when I sit around and talk to them, that there's a space there.

There's a void, a kind of emptiness. I can always focus back and say I'm glad I was part of that process.

Other experience was important, but not equivalent to the movement that I was engaged in from '62 through '65. It's almost as if everything else is a footnote. There was a sense of mission, a sense of correctness, a sense of change. Not only were we transforming ourselves and our lives, but we were also transforming the lives of our parents. My father and mother went on to vote. My father eventually ran for alderman in Holly Springs. He did not win, but he ran. My father wouldn't have dreamed of that in the sixties. My brother is now vice mayor of Holly Springs. It's because of those changes. It's because of the risks people took.

Sheyann Webb listens to Dr. Martin Luther King, Jr., preach.

7. *Bloody Sunday and the Selma Movement*

In 1965 the civil rights battleground shifted to Selma, Alabama, a former slave market town, about fifty miles from Montgomery. Nearly half the voting-age population in the Selma area was black, but only one percent was registered to vote. That meant some 150 blacks were registered out of about 15,000 who were eligible.

Black people repeatedly attempted to sign up at the county courthouse, but were as repeatedly turned away and sometimes arrested by Sheriff Jim Clark and his police "possemen." As in most other southern towns, when blacks were allowed to take the tests, they were seldom passed.

In the early sixties, local activists and SNCC volunteers set up voter registration workshops. Sheriff Clark would harass them, sending officers to meetings to record the names of those who attended. Then he'd release the names to newspapers in the hope that the civil rights "agitators" would be fired from their jobs.

In the mid-sixties SCLC workers began to organize in Selma. Their goals were twofold: desegregate stores and other public facilities, and register voters. Young activists from nearby Montgomery came to help. Sixteen-year-old Princella Howard went to Selma with James Orange from the SCLC staff in late August 1964. She has a vivid memory of that event:

> I can remember driving into Selma at night. It was dark. Ooh, I remember how black dark it was. The SCLC office had heard there was a movement starting there. They wanted us to see if it looked like something vital enough that we could work around the issue of voting rights and build a movement.
>
> We went to SNCC's office, which was already set up, to see what they were doing and what they thought. They said this was the next place . . . this is it!
>
> Then we went to a church meeting. It was as

black as could be outside, but when that church door swung open and we went in, it was like a bright light. I could see a glow in that church. It was the most unusual night. It was as bright and fired up in that church as it was dark outside. Whatever these people are praying for, they got it. That's how I looked at it. It was a-moaning and a-groaning, and it was some deep prayer going on in that church.

In January and February 1965, Martin Luther King came to Selma. Every day SCLC organized marches to the courthouse and to downtown stores, and every evening television news covered the mass arrests. When Dr. King was arrested, he observed that "there are more Negroes in jail with me than there are on the voting rolls."

One evening Reverend C. T. Vivian of SCLC spoke at a mass meeting in nearby Marion, Alabama. As the audience left the church for a nighttime march, police troopers and a local mob attacked the crowd. Many people were wounded, including news reporters. Twenty-seven-year-old Jimmie Lee Jackson, a native of Marion, was fatally shot while trying to protect his mother from a beating by state troopers. He died eight days later.

Dr. King spoke at Jackson's funeral. He said that Jackson had been murdered by police "in the name of the law," by politicians who feed their listeners "the stale bread of hatred and the spoiled meat of racism," by a government that wouldn't "protect the lives of its own citizens seeking the right to vote," and by "every Negro who passively accepts the evils of segregation and stands on the sidelines in the struggle for justice."

Reverend James Bevel of SCLC called for a fifty-mile march from Selma to the capital in Montgomery to protest Jackson's murder and to demand full voting rights for blacks. Alabama governor George Wallace opposed the march; a demonstration protesting a police killing would receive national news coverage and would be bad publicity for Alabama. He announced that state troopers would block the march.

The march organizers did not back down. On Sunday morning, March 7, 1965, hundreds left Brown Chapel, unofficial headquarters of the Selma movement. They headed for the Edmund Pettus Bridge, where they were met by state troopers and local police. The marchers never got out of the Selma city limits. The troopers viciously beat them in a police riot that came to be known as Bloody Sunday.

Television stations all over America interrupted their local programs to show footage of the police riot. President Johnson said at a news conference, "What happened in Selma was an American tragedy." Later, in an address to Congress, the president asked for passage of a voting rights act, saying, "Their cause must be our cause, too. Because it's not just Negroes, but it's really all of us who must overcome the crippling legacy of bigotry and injustice." He ended his speech with the words of the civil rights song: "We shall overcome!"

After Bloody Sunday, Dr. King made a national appeal, asking clergy from around the country to come to Selma to join a second march. Not only clergy answered the call. Thousands of people, white and black, poured into the city. They slept on couches, floors, anywhere there was room. SCLC went to court to seek an order preventing Governor Wallace from stopping the second march. When the court finally ruled in favor of the marchers, President Johnson federalized the Alabama National Guard, thereby placing them under federal, not state, government control, and sent two thousand U.S. army troops, one hundred FBI agents and one hundred federal marshals to line the highway route to protect the marchers.

Princella Howard was attending college in Iowa at the time of Bloody Sunday. As president of the college and youth division of the Iowa NAACP, she was sent back home to join the second march.

When I was on the train coming from Sioux City, there were loads of young ministerial white students on that train. As we got closer to Montgomery and I realized that they hadn't gotten off, the exchanges started. When I found out that they were coming to the Selma march, I got so excited. I said, ''Show me who you're going to talk to and what numbers you have to call when you get there.'' The man pulled out his purse and guess whose phone number it was? Mine! I said, ''That's my mother!'' MIA had only so many phone lines, and all of a sudden all of these people from all over the world were coming. So they opened up private phones on the street nearby. Ours was one of the first ones they used because of course we had been in the movement all of our lives.

You can imagine how excited I was. You see, the movement was my life. When I had to go away to college, it was one of the hardest things I've ever done—to break away from the movement. It was a real strong family in the movement. Even now I don't think anybody who was outside the movement really realizes it. They were very strong, powerful cords. I mean, once you're in, you're in for life.

Thousands gathered on the morning of March 21 at Brown Chapel in Selma. They walked during the day and camped at night along the highway until they arrived four days later at St. Jude's school grounds in Montgomery. That night they held a big rally with entertainers Harry Belafonte, Tony Bennett, Joan Baez and others. Gladis Williams, a high school student, worked in the Montgomery Improvement Association office preparing for the arrival of the marchers from Selma.

I was on the MIA welcoming committee. We had to register all the people who were coming into town. They were coming from all over the nation, so we had a housing committee assigning them to homes. A lot came down to be in Montgomery when the march arrived here, and a lot of them went on to Selma to go on the march. We were collecting blankets and food for the marchers.

The day of the march, the school principal locked all the doors and all the windows because kids were jumping out of the windows trying to get to the march. I didn't go to school that day. It's important to go to school, but it was also important during that time for us to deal with the different problems that were here in Montgomery. It was just something we had to do.

When the marchers arrived from Selma, we were there to greet them. Thousands were there. Joy! That's what you felt. They stopped at St. Jude's, and that's where they camped out that night. They had come fifty miles, but when you're marching and singing, it doesn't faze you how far it is.

The next day at least twenty-five thousand people marched through the city to the steps of the capital. A delegation from the group presented a petition to an aide of the governor, demanding an end to voting rights restrictions.

Delores Boyd was in the tenth grade. "It was just glorious walking down Dexter Avenue. There were troopers, folks on horses, and whites who were taunting. But there were so many black folk and white folk who joined the march. It was just such a lovely sight."

But there were sacrifices along with the triumph. Both blacks and whites were killed. The first to die had been Jimmie Lee Jackson. Then James Reeb, a white minister from Boston who had answered Dr. King's call for clergy volunteers, was clubbed to death by a group of whites as he and his companions left a restaurant in Selma. At the end of the second march, there was a third killing. Viola Liuzzo, a white homemaker from Detroit, had seen the Bloody Sunday police riot on television. She then drove down to Selma to participate in the demonstrations. On Thursday, March 25, at the end of the rally in Montgomery, she drove marchers back to their homes in Selma. On a return trip to Montgomery, a carload of Klansmen spotted her Michigan license plates. They pulled alongside her on the highway and shot her through the car window.

Mary Gadson, from Birmingham, recalls the reaction of the community:

When Viola Liuzzo was killed, it was like she was a part of the family. I never knew her more than her name and that she was a Freedom Rider. But even today she's like a part of the family. That's just how much unity there was. During that time I believe she was a part of all black families. She really became kinfolks because she was involved. Her race didn't make a difference. To me she was a human being who was concerned, who had a heart, and who gave her life for what she believed in.

The sacrifices were not empty losses. Barbara Howard, who organized her Montgomery classmates to join the Selma marchers when they reached the capital, said:

The Selma murders were a real sadness. How could people take a life? They could see that they were losing the battle. They could see at this point we were halfway home. From 1955 up to 1965 a lot of ground had been covered and a lot of momentum had been built. So it only strengthened us. They didn't know that through the murders they actually helped to bring about the change faster than it would have come. And the nonviolence on our part moved it more smoothly.

As a result of the Selma demonstrations, President Johnson urged passage of a law to protect voting rights, which Congress passed later that year. Under the law, federal, not state or local, officials conducted registration. The law suspended literacy tests and other discriminatory voting rules, and provided for federal government oversight of election procedures to prevent discrimination.

Some people believe that the Voting Rights Act of 1965 has had the most far-reaching effect of any civil rights legislation in promoting equality for blacks in America. In Selma the effect was clear. The year after the act was passed, over nine thousand blacks registered and then voted Sheriff Jim Clark out of office.

SHEYANN WEBB

Sheyann Webb was eight years old when she became a civil rights activist. She grew up in the housing project next to Brown Chapel AME Church in Selma.

I am the seventh child of eight, and I'm the baby girl. We were very poor, living in the George Washington Carver homes.

My house was right behind the Brown Chapel AME Church. The civil rights movement in Selma really began at this church. I had to pass it to go to school, and this is where I played most of the time. I remember this particular morning, on my way to school, seeing something that was different. A lot of blacks and whites mingling together. That was unusual to me. I used to see black people sitting together, and whites where they were supposed to be. I had never seen them in a friendly or social environment where they were actually communicating.

As I began to cross the street, I was still watching and wondering what was going on. I looked back and saw them as they began to go into the church. I was so wondering about that, I decided I'd cross back over and follow behind them. I didn't think about what might happen if I was late to school. It didn't even cross my mind. I went into church and sat in the last pew in the back. I began to listen to what the people were saying on the pulpit. I remember Hosea Williams being the presiding officer that day. He began to talk about blacks in Selma not being registered voters. He talked about the numbers, how many blacks weren't registered. He talked about Dr. Martin Luther King. I didn't know anything about any of these things, but it was something that seemed exciting. It was like something was about to happen.

Finally I left and went on to school. When I got there, I realized I might be punished. I was very afraid to go into my classroom. I stood outside, and my teacher saw me peeking in. She told me to come in and she asked me in front of the classroom where I had been. I began to try to whisper to her and explain. The more I talked to her about what I saw and what I had heard, it became more interesting to her. I realized later on why. It was because at that time teachers weren't even registered. It was a time when nothing was happening in Selma in terms of the struggle.

As I talked she began to ask me question after question. Most questions I couldn't even answer. She told me they would have to contact my parents. And then she said I had no business being over there in that mess. As the day went on, I could see her whispering to other teachers about what I had told her.

When I got home that afternoon, of course they had talked with my mom and dad. All I could think about was being whipped. Then I began to see how inquisitive they were as they talked to me about what was going on. It made my parents nervous not only for me, but about what was about to happen in Selma. They were fearing something. This made it even more interesting to me.

I wanted to know about voting. I didn't know what that was about. And then I wanted to know who was this man Dr. Martin Luther King. Once Hosea Williams talked about him coming to Selma, you could tell in his expression and the way the people were applauding that he had to be somebody great. My parents knew of his name, but it was like I shouldn't know him or want to know him. This made me even more inquisitive. I was told to stay away from around there. I had no business being there.

Rachel, who was my best friend, lived right next door. After I saw I wasn't going to get a whipping, I was anxious to tell her about what happened. We talked, and I told her I was going back out there.

One day we were playing out in front of the church, and we saw some pretty cars drive up. In the sixties in our housing area, we didn't see many big cars ride through there like that. It caught our attention. We saw these black men get out of the cars, all dressed neat. And we saw them as they huddled and were talking among themselves. We went a little closer, and when we got near them, there was this man who spoke to us and asked us our names. We told him, and he told us his. That was Dr. King. I said to Rachel, "This is the man that they were talking about!" So we followed them all into the church.

There was this other man who said to us, "You all can go on now." Dr. King immediately told him, "No, let them stay. There's nothing we can do to harm them." So we went on inside and sat there.

Then before they got ready to leave, Dr. King came

to us again and told us that he wanted to see us when he came back. This was exciting to us, especially to me, because this was the man Hosea Williams had been talking about. Just the idea that he had the patience. He didn't throw us aside, or anything. He gave us the attention.

I didn't start learning what freedom meant until later on. We went home and told our parents that we met Dr. Martin Luther King, and that they were talking about a mass meeting, whatever that was. It was going to be at Brown Chapel Church, and I wanted to be there.

It started off with Rachel and me going to mass meetings. We'd sit in the front row and sing. The first song we learned was "Ain't Gonna Let Nobody Turn Me 'Round." That song itself told me a lot about what freedom was. It naturally meant there was going to be a struggle for rights that were owed to the black race.

The more mass meetings I attended, the more I began to learn. The words equality and justice were mentioned so much. I put all the pieces together just with those words. I may not have understood it well, but I understood enough.

It was so visible with us being there as children, that they started asking us to come up and lead freedom songs. When Dr. Martin Luther King had first come to one of the mass meetings, we were sitting in the front row. We had already led a few freedom songs, and we inched up to the pulpit and sat on his lap. He remembered us, and every time he would come, we would go up there and sit on his lap. We looked forward to him being there. It was just a thrill. The more we saw him come, the more mass meetings I attended. I became a very disobedient child. That's how deep I got into it.

Teachers were afraid for a long time because they would definitely lose their jobs if they had got involved in any way. They would call on me sometimes just to ask me what was going on. It was a great day when I saw all of the teachers marching together. That was a beautiful day.

Before then I only recall one teacher that stood out among all of them. Her name was Margaret Moore. After I had made my own decision that I was going to do it anyway, even though my parents said not to, this is the lady I would look to, Margaret Moore. On the demonstrations I would always go with her. I felt I was safe then. She was not my teacher. She was a teacher at another school.

I remember the first march I went on very well. I had gone to a mass meeting, and they were talking about marching to the Dallas County courthouse. It was a march about blacks getting registered to vote, and you had to register at the courthouse. I wasn't sure that I really wanted to go because it just wasn't clear what could happen. But I also wanted to be there. As I got ready for school, this was on my mind. I stopped at the church.

After I had gotten there and they began to prepare to march, I got with Margaret Moore. It was exciting to me, seeing all the people walking. We sang as we marched. Looking at the hostility, now that was a little frightening. You could see it and feel it as you walked. You know, whites standing at the side and looking and saying nasty things. I remember the policemen having their billy clubs. On this one march we went to a certain point, and we prayed and then turned back around.

With my family, it was always that fear factor. This lasted a long time. Everything that I saw and everything that I really wanted to talk about was almost being pushed aside. I recall one time as I really began to grow into the movement, coming and talking to my mom about what they were saying at the meetings. I remember her telling me that I could cause her to lose her job. I didn't understand that, and I began to ask her how could she lose her job with me being there. "White folks don't like that. If they knew that you were involved and you're my child, they would fire me."

But I didn't have any fear. I used to tell my momma, "I want you and Daddy to be free. I want you to be able to vote just like the white folks." They couldn't do it. They just couldn't do it. "We ain't free. We're not gonna be free." This really made me be motivated more and more.

My parents had given me the example of the four girls killed in the church bombing in Birmingham to keep me from being involved. They said it could happen in Selma at Brown Chapel Church. And there were several bomb threats.

Why children? Why us? It made me realize that it didn't matter who you were. If you were black and you were in an area they didn't like or where the cause for freedom was being fought, you were at risk. It didn't matter—children, boy, girl, or whatever.

My father and I went to Jimmie Lee Jackson's funeral. There were a number of situations that I knew of as a kid where death actually happened. Jimmie Lee Jackson, James Reeb, Jonathan Daniels, Viola

Liuzzo, the four kids in Birmingham. Three of the people were white, but they were part of the struggle. And in the struggle it didn't matter if you were black or white, we were all just like a big family.

I remember being afraid on the first attempt of the Selma-to-Montgomery march [March 7, 1965]. That was the first time that I was really afraid. The night before the march I slipped to the mass meeting. They began to talk about the strategies, like not fighting back. That right there told me that there was a possibility that there could be some fights. They were saying if you're hit, or if something is said to you, just bow down. Out of all the times my parents had talked to me about what could happen, this is when it really came to me. But somehow I was still determined to go.

I got up the next morning, frightened to march. This was on a Sunday. I remember very well my mom and dad trying to ensure that I was in the house. I slipped out the back door and I ran down.

The people began to congregate and line up. I was looking for Mrs. Moore and I found her. I remember not wanting to get close to the front of the line because I was afraid. I remember Mrs. Moore telling me that I should go back home, and I was saying I was going to march. I got in the midway of the march. As usual we knelt down to pray, and after we had prayed, we began to sing. A little of that fear began to leave me as we sang, because people were still joyful.

As we marched down the street to the downtown area, I began to see more spectators, black as well as whites, and this was different to me. Normally you didn't see a whole lot of spectators. And I began to see more police officers riding around on motorcycles. It was a little bit more exciting. We still clapped, and we sang all the way down. The closer we got to the bridge, the more I began to get frightened. At this time I could see hundreds of policemen. The helmets, state troopers, dogs and horses, police cars. I got even more frightened then. I began to hold Mrs. Moore's hand tighter, and the person's hand on the other side of me. My heart was beginning to beat real, real fast. I looked up at Mrs. Moore, and I wanted to say, "I want to go home," but I didn't. She was looking straight ahead. Then the people began to kneel down and pray again.

We were still on the Edmund Pettus bridge. Going up, you can't see what's at the bottom on the other side. But I had gotten up to the top, which is midway on the bridge, and you could see down. The big picture that I saw frightened me more. When we were asked to kneel down and pray, I knelt down with everybody. Shortly after we got up, a burst of tear gas began. I could see the troopers and policemen swinging their billy clubs. People began to run, and dogs and horses began to trample them. You could hear people screaming and hollering. And I began to run. I don't know what happened with Mrs. Moore. All I wanted to do was make my way back home. As I got almost down to the bottom of the bridge, Hosea Williams picked me up. I told him to put me down 'cause he wasn't running fast enough. I just continued to run.

You began to hear sirens. You could still see the dogs and horses trampling people, who were running all the way back from the Edmund Pettus bridge to Brown Chapel Church. When I made my way back home, I saw my mother and father and even my sisters and brothers there. My father was standing in the doorway. They were just waiting for me to get home. I remember him opening up the door and taking a deep breath seeing me, that I was safe. I went straight upstairs. He stood at the door watching what else was happening after I had come in. I was crying, and my mother came upstairs to comfort me. I was shocked at what I had seen.

I was still determined to go back out to Brown Chapel Church, but my parents wouldn't let me. I was shut up in my room. I remember taking a pencil and writing down how I felt and what I saw. Then I wrote down my funeral arrangements because even with what I saw, I still wanted to go out and fight. And I said if I did that, I would probably die. So I wrote my funeral arrangements.

I realized on that day everything about what Dr. Martin Luther King was trying to say. It was wrong to be beaten for something that you was trying to fight for that was right. I realized it more on that day than on any other day. It all came together.

I didn't get out that night, but I went to the next meeting, and this is when other people who hadn't the slightest idea of getting involved in the movement came to get involved. It had made so many people angry about what took place in Selma on that day, that it really helped mobilize and bring blacks together.

Meetings after that were filled with people. They were fired up. Teachers, the ministers, the grass roots from all walks of life. People began to come from all over the world. I remember the first mass meeting my parents came to. My mom and dad, they were telling me that they were gonna come to one of the mass meetings. I was already there, and it was a great thrill for me to look back and see them. Then after they had gone to the meeting, we talked about them getting registered to vote. They promised me for my birthday that they would be registered. That was going to be my birthday present.

The second Selma-to-Montgomery march began on March 21, 1965. Sheyann participated.

It was almost like preparing for a picnic. I remember getting some sandwiches. I still wasn't supposed to be on that march. When I saw Dr. King, he asked me who was I with, and I said, "Nobody." So immediately I was in his group's care. They put me in a van and I came on over to Montgomery with one of his secretaries. Dr. King told his assistant that my parents had to be contacted and told that I was in their care, and that I was okay.

We went to this hotel up on a hill. It was my first time going in a hotel. We were sitting in the hotel room, and they had asked me what I wanted to eat. I didn't know what to tell them. They said, "Get her a club sandwich." I didn't know what a club sandwich was. It was the biggest sandwich I had ever seen, and it was with chips and a pickle.

I felt I was part of the change. Really, anyone who was a part of the struggle at that time contributed to a change. So I think anyone, young or old, who participated in the movement was a contributing factor to the good things that are happening as a result of the Selma movement.

But now [25 years later], right here in Selma where the struggle actually took place, it looks like voter registration is declining. There are a lot of reasons why people don't vote. Some people say they don't like who's running, but that's not the point. When I went to register, that was something I looked forward to. When I go vote, I probably don't feel like most people feel. When I pull the switch, I just feel good about it. It's like a proud thing to me because I know what happened for us to get that.

JAWANA JACKSON

Jawana Jackson was four and a half years old at the time of the Selma demonstrations in 1965. Martin Luther King, Jr., stayed in her house whenever he was in Selma.

My direct involvement started when Dr. King and the movement came into Selma. He was introduced to me as Uncle Martin, and calling him Uncle Martin was just a natural thing.

There was never a time that he was in Selma that he wasn't at my house. I think it was very logical for him to go to my parents', because if anybody could lend any support, it would be someone who was on their own, self-employed, and didn't have to rely on the system. My father was a dentist.

When our house was taken over by the movement, that was when I sensed something's going on here. Prior to that, I was just a normal child, and it was just the three of us in a house. After that, I would get shuffled to my grandmother's on a regular basis, often in the middle of the night. I can remember getting wrapped up in blankets and sheets and sleeping wherever I could sleep. There was an alley behind our house, and if we couldn't get out by car, some of the men that worked with Dr. King would just shuffle me down the alley, and nobody would know what was going on. Then somebody could pick me up and get me to other parts of the city.

Both my parents asked me to kind of hold fast. They said they were doing some things to ensure my future. You can't explain to a four-year-old about legislation and slavery and hard times. All you can do is say things are hectic right now. I got the standard teaching that there are going to be some people out here that think that you're different, but you're not. They never really said "not as good as." I think that was their way of not even planting that in my mind. I knew they meant white people. Even when I would say to Uncle Martin, "What's going on?" his thing was, "We're doing this to help you and all of the little children."

In comes the movement. The front door bell would ring, and I saw lots of people. I was always short, so I could go under tables and chairs. I would get to the front door, and there would always be some adults over me. To a child, adults are giants. I saw a gentleman in a fantastic garb. He had a huge white beard. It was Archbishop Makarios from Cyprus, who had come over to talk with Dr. King about the movement and religion. I would see figures such as Benjamin Mays [president of Morehouse College]. I would say, "Why all these people?" and I'd take all of these questions either to my mother or Uncle Martin or whoever happened to be around at the time. They all said that it was to ensure my well-being for the years to come.

I realized that some powerful things were going on. I remember sessions, staff meetings, and powwows that would go on all through the night. Nobody ever kept me out. I was free to roam. Those sessions were so intense. I remember that.

Those roads from Montgomery to Atlanta and Selma were traveled so frequently by movement people. It was just something you did. Usually Uncle Martin would have a driver, but on a couple of occasions he came by himself. It would infuriate my mother and father. They would speak to him quite harshly about it. "Don't come driving down these roads by yourself, Martin. It makes no sense." He would just throw it off. "Well, I had to get here, and I didn't want anyone driving me. I just want peace." But it would tear all of us up. They were afraid for his safety.

The Klan was out in front of the house. They just set up camp there. The number of Klan varied, but they were there as many days as Uncle Martin was there.

In the dining room there's one whole wall that's windows. Uncle Martin used to sit at the head of the dining room table, and if you sit there, your back is to all the windows. We had gotten a tip one evening that someone was going to shoot him. My father was frantic. "Martin, there's some crackpot out here that's fixing to kill you." He marched in one of the bedrooms and got the gun. Uncle Martin and Daddy used to always get into this dialogue about nonviolence. It would always end with Uncle Martin chuckling, saying, "Sully, you're just such a great human being, but I'm just not going to be able to convert you."

When this incident happened, and my father went immediately to arm himself, Uncle Martin put his arm on Daddy's shoulder and said, "If I'm to go like this, so be it. We're not going to take any extra precau-

tions.'' Everybody was trying to get him to move. At
least go into the living room. He just sat there and
continued his meeting. The night turned out to be un-
eventful.

*Dr. King and his aides organized at Jawana's
house for the second march from Selma to Montgomery on March 21.*

I went stumbling into this bedroom, and there was
Uncle Martin, Uncle Ralph [Abernathy], Andy
[Young], Bernard Lee, [James] Bevel, all of his closest people. Whenever they got ready to do major
things, all of this group came together.

They had stayed at my house that night. Everybody.
They had the doors closed on this one, but I just went
barging in. They were huddled and praying. I stood
there for a few moments, and they came up out of
prayer.

I can remember one evening when the telephone was
ringing off the hook. Uncle Martin was there, and
President Johnson's operator was trying to get
through. Someone was on the phone, and they interrupted it. He finally got through to Uncle Martin.
Now, that was an experience, because my mother let
me know Uncle Martin was talking to the president
of the United States. I remember standing there, just
looking at him.

When I was five or six, I besieged my parents with
questions. And then they talked to me. They went all
the way back and talked about slavery. This was the
number-one question that came to my mind about the
whole issue: I asked my mother, ''At what moment

did the white man decide that he could be over everybody?'' She wasn't able to give me an answer. Nobody's been able to give me an answer.

TOWANNER HINKLE

Towanner Hinkle grew up in Selma. She was sixteen years old when she marched in the Selma demonstrations of 1965.

The movement had started, and we heard that Dr. King was coming to town. We were excited about that. We knew that he was a brilliant man, and that he believed in nonviolence. We were attending R. B. Hudson High School at the time. We'd leave home like we're going to school. Ride the bus, get off, and head straight to Brown Chapel Church. Then they would tell us what to do. Brown Chapel was our home. That's where we started at, that's where we lined up at, that's where we would march from.

At the mass meetings adult leader Marie Foster would give a fifteen-minute talk about black history, as she said, "to give the young people self-esteem, to let them know they were somebody. Just because they weren't in the history books, that didn't mean that they were nobody."

We learned a lot at the meetings. I remember Mrs. Foster's lessons. In school class our teacher would tell us nasty things about black people. But at the church meetings Mrs. Foster talked about us being human beings and to pay no mind to old stereotypes.

I lived with my aunt. She said, "I don't want you in jail because you'll have a record the rest of your life.'' She was worried I'd get killed. Those kids had got bombed in Birmingham [1963]. I said, ''Mama, I'm going.''

They would send six of us to go to different places. We'd go to the stores and try putting in applications for jobs. They gave us a test. Never was called. Always said you didn't pass the test. The next time we had a mass meeting, we would go and report what we had done.

On one demonstration they said to us, ''If you march, you're going to jail.'' Police were standing all down the street with the billy clubs. We were singing ''We Shall Overcome.'' That was our main song. We marched, and they carried us to jail. They piled us in anything that they could find. We were still singing. Sheriff Jim Clark said, ''No damn singing, no damn praying!'' Oh, he was low-down.

When we got to jail, we asked for some water and Jim Clark says, ''No damn water!'' He got a great big tub and set it in the middle of the jail cell. Then he said, ''You niggers want to act like cows and dogs, that's the way we're going to treat you.'' That tub of water was for all of us to drink. We stayed in jail three days like that.

You could stand up on the beds in the jail and holler out at someone passing, ''Tell my mother I'm here.'' My aunt almost had a heart attack. She raised me from two years old. My grandmother and my uncle, they died, so it was just the two of us. She was upset, oh yes, Lord. She was afraid they were going to bomb the jail, or beat us half to death.

Our mayor was then and still is Joe T. Smitherman. And we had a classmate named Joe T. Smitherman. Jim Clark said, ''Nigger, what's your name?''

Joe said, ''Joseph T. Smitherman.''

"Nigger, I'm gonna ask you again, what is your name?"

"Joseph T. Smitherman." So Jim Clark went and got a big block of ice and sat Joe on it. Almost beat him to death, until Reverend Reese came up there and told them that his name *was* Joseph T. Smitherman.

I went to jail a lot. We marched downtown because we were tired. Tired of going in Kress's and you could order something, but you had to take it outside. We were tired of that. We were tired of being put in the back all the time. When we went to the movies, they had a colored side and a white side. The white side was always better. We were tired of this.

There were no black young ladies working like it is now in the grocery stores. There were no jobs. Only whites were getting the best jobs. We used to say, "What's the use of going to school? Let's drop out." At a meeting someone said, "I want you all to stay in school. I want you all to get an education because you're gonna need it after this movement is over." And he was absolutely right.

We would have different leaders come in. They would give us words of encouragement and march with us. They would say, "Things are going to get better, but you're just going to have to fight, fight, fight. If you go to jail, we'll get you out. They want us to give up, but you must keep on."

I didn't go on Bloody Sunday [March 7], but I went on the second march [March 21]. A lot of kids went. We even had some of the teachers, though they would jeopardize their jobs. I didn't make it all the way to Montgomery. I got up to Hayneville, near where Viola Liuzzo was killed. I slept on the road two nights, and then the bus brought us home. I wanted to go all the way, but they said our parents were worried, so we had to go back.

You know, it's a wonder any one of us is living. They were so cruel then. I feel that if Lyndon Baines Johnson hadn't done what he did, there's no telling what would have happened to us in Selma. I mean the protection on the march, with the state troopers and the federal men.

When we were marching, some people said doing this and going to jail was going to follow us the rest of our lives. I've had interviews for jobs and they say, "Have you ever been to jail?"

I say, "Yes, I've been to jail a lot of times." They look at me real funny. And I say, "I went to jail for marching with the movement."

"Oh, don't even worry about that," they say.

I think if I hadn't marched, if I hadn't witnessed what I've seen for myself, I wouldn't have the strength I have today. There are a lot of drugs today in Selma. If I hadn't been in the movement, there's a possibility I could be on drugs. It was rough in those days, much rougher than it is now. It made me strong. It gave me encouragement. When I see things now that are going wrong, I can speak out about it and let them know I don't like it.

When I reached voting age, the first place I went was the courthouse. I walked in there with pride, you hear me? I was so proud to say I want to register to vote. I'm a deputy registrar now. I can register people that's out in the community. And I work at the voting place when elections come around. When a person comes in to vote, I know what we went through to become registered voters.

At the funeral of Dr. Martin Luther King, Jr.

Epilogue

On April 4, 1968, Dr. Martin Luther King, Jr. was assassinated in Memphis, Tennessee. He had gone there to help the garbage workers, who were striking for a pay increase. He had planned to lead a nonviolent march with them. The night before he was killed, he gave a speech in which he talked about the death threats he had received.

> Like anybody, I would like to live a long life. Longevity has its place. But I'm not concerned

167

about that now. I just want to do God's will. And
He's allowed me to go up to the mountain. And
I've looked over, and I've seen the promised
land. I may not get there with you. But I want
you to know tonight that we as a people will get
to the promised land. So I'm happy tonight. I'm
not worried about anything. I'm not fearing any
man. Mine eyes have seen the glory of the coming of the Lord.

That was to be Dr. King's last speech.

His murder the next day stunned the nation and the
world. In some communities there were riots; in others, simply deep grieving. Young southern blacks felt
they had lost a leader, a colleague, a friend.

━━━━▭

Thelma Eubanks was in Mississippi.

When we heard he was shot, everybody was devas-
tated. We felt we had lost probably the only black
man who had guts enough to be as brave as he was.
We felt a big loss. We felt there was not going to be
another King, not like him. We felt angry, but we
knew that he would eventually get killed. Anybody
who stepped out during that bad time when whites
could get away with anything, southern whites, oh,
we knew he was going to get killed. We had accepted
it. We just didn't know when.

*In Selma, Alabama, Jawana Jackson heard the
news on television.*

We had just finished supper. During those years, everyone got the news at the dinner hour. That's how you knew how many people died in Vietnam that day. We were getting up from the table and the sign "Special Report" flashed. And for some reason my mother said, "Martin's dead." This was in the second between the news flash sign coming on and the commentator talking. It was uncanny. The next words he said were, "We have gotten a confirmed report that Martin Luther King, Jr. has been assassinated in Memphis."

The three of us just looked at each other. That was the hardest night we ever spent in the house. We just walked around and didn't talk to each other. The next day we got a telegram from Coretta, confirming that it had happened and that she'd be in touch about a formal private wake.

I felt shock. Uncle Martin? Dead? In the next couple of days, we came to Atlanta. Looking at that man in the casket was unbelievable. To see someone that I had known, who had had as much life as he had, to be lifeless. He was just no more. I didn't know who to be angry at. I just knew he was dead, and it was over.

As if speaking for all who mourned, Arlam Carr, a high school senior in Montgomery, Alabama, demanded public recognition of the tragedy.

The day Martin Luther King was killed, I didn't see the flag at half-staff at school. I walked into the auditorium and in anger threw my books down. Then I walked to the principal's office and I said, "Why isn't the flag at half-staff?" He said that flag-raising was the responsibility of the ROTC program. So I turned right around and walked down the hall to the ROTC room.

Normally when you wanted to see the major, you had to say, "Sergeant Carr requests permission to see Major such and such." I just walked past the sergeant, right into the major's office. I said, "Why is the flag at full-staff? It's supposed to be flown at half-staff. The president of the United States said all flags are supposed to be flown at half-staff."

He said, "Okay, Arlam, we will get it taken care of." I walked out front and waited with this other guy who was also a senior. I had made up my mind that if it was not at half-staff by the time the first bell rang, we were going to take it completely down.

I felt that they weren't giving Dr. King the respect that he was due. Hey, you know, here in Montgomery, Alabama, is where he started. This is the place where every flag should have been at half-staff without having to be asked. Oh, I was very angry!

The funeral was on a school day. I wanted to go. My mother wrote a note to the school saying there was a death in the family. I remember we were at a church in Atlanta across the street from where the funeral was. The horse and wagon went by. You could see the coffin and people walking behind it.

When I got back to school the next day, a lot of kids said, "I heard so-and-so came to school." I said, "I'm not worried about who came to school. If they came, that's fine. If they can't give up a day out of school for a man who's given his life for the things that we have gotten, that's their problem. They have to live with that, I don't."

Sheyann Webb came home from a ballet class in Selma and found her family listening to the tele-

vision news. When the bulletin came that King was dead, she said she could "hear people responding in the community. You could hear it through the walls."

I began to get a whole lot of mixed emotions about what I was taught by him. I was very angry. I was feeling violent. I had the feeling that I hated all whites after he was killed. It was like killing a person that was really holding us together.

I came out of it. I began to really get involved in me. It made me want to be somebody. It was a slow process, but I began to see and realize more what he was trying to say. Then as I grew older, I got into a competitive thing with whites. I didn't go to an all-black school like my brothers and sisters. I went to a predominately white school. This is junior high and high school. I was willing to stay in that struggle. I was the only black in most of my classes. I was spat on and called "nigger," but Dr. King had taught me how to deal with that.

One thing that stuck in me that Dr. King used to always say: If he couldn't risk his life to fight for his people, then there wasn't no reason for him to live. That just kept coming to mind. I knew what he had done. I knew what I had seen, what I had heard from him. It was like he was fighting a battle for us and he died for it.

Dr. King, of course, was not the only person to give his life in the fight for civil rights. At least forty others also died in the 1950s and 1960s. Nor did the movement end with his death. But by then the southern nonviolent movement as described in these pages had peaked, and the bat-

tleground was shifting to northern urban areas.

The decade from 1955 to 1965 had been an extraordinary time in the South and in the country as a whole. There were thousands of young people like those who have told their stories in these pages. Collectively, it is one story of a movement for rights and justice that was forcing the segregated South to undergo painful change. These young activists were transformed by this movement, and by their involvement they transformed the lives of those around them.

Chronology

This is a selected chronology of the major events that are referred to in this book.

1954   MAY 17.   The United States Supreme Court declares school segregation to be unconstitutional in the case *Brown v. Board of Education of Topeka.*

The first Citizen's Council is formed by whites in Mississippi to block school integration.

1955   MARCH 2.   Claudette Colvin, a teenager, is arrested in Montgomery, Alabama, for refusing to give up her bus seat to a white person.

MAY 7.   In Belzoni, Mississippi, Reverend George Lee, active in the National Association for the Advancement of Colored People (NAACP), is murdered for his voter registration activities.

AUGUST 28.   Emmett Till, a Chicago teenager visiting relatives in Mississippi, is tortured and

killed for allegedly talking to a white woman
in an "improper" way.

NOVEMBER.   The Interstate Commerce Com-
mission bans segregated buses and waiting
rooms for interstate travel. Most white southern communities ignore the order.

DECEMBER 1.   Rosa Parks is arrested in
Montgomery for the same action Claudette
Colvin had taken—refusing to give up her bus
seat to a white person.

DECEMBER 5.   The Montgomery Bus Boycott
begins and lasts over a year, until the buses
are integrated. The Montgomery Improvement
Association (MIA) is formed to coordinate the
boycott, and Dr. Martin Luther King, Jr. is
elected president.

1956   MARCH 12.   Nearly a hundred Congressional
Representatives and Senators sign the "South-
ern Manifesto," vowing to fight the Supreme
Court school desegregation decision.

JUNE.   Alabama outlaws the NAACP. In Birmingham, Reverend Fred Shuttlesworth organizes the Alabama Christian Movement for
Human Rights (ACMHR) to carry on civil
rights activities.

NOVEMBER.   The United States Supreme
Court rules that Montgomery bus segregation
laws are unconstitutional. On December 21 the

boycott ends in victory and the buses are integrated.

DECEMBER 25. The Shuttlesworth home in Birmingham is bombed.

1957 JANUARY. The Southern Christian Leadership Conference (SCLC, originally with another name) is founded. Martin Luther King, Jr. becomes its president.

AUGUST. Two students, Ricky and Pat Shuttlesworth, attempt to integrate all-white Phillips High School in Birmingham. They and their parents are attacked by a violent white mob.

SEPTEMBER. Arkansas governor Orval Faubus orders the National Guard to keep nine black students from integrating Little Rock's Central High School. President Eisenhower orders the 101st Airborne Division to Little Rock to protect the Little Rock Nine.

1958 MAY. Ernest Green becomes the first black student to graduate from Little Rock's Central High School. The following school year, Arkansas governor Orval Faubus closes all public schools in Little Rock to prevent further integration.

1960 FEBRUARY. Sit-ins by black students at segregated facilities begin in Greensboro, North Carolina. Similar protests take place all over the South and in some northern communities.

APRIL. More than a hundred students from nine states meet at Shaw University in North Carolina and form the Student Nonviolent Coordinating Committee (SNCC).

1961   MAY. Freedom Riders organized by the Congress of Racial Equality (CORE) travel on buses from Washington D.C. headed for Alabama and Mississippi to challenge local segregated travel rules. The buses are attacked on May 14 outside of Anniston, Alabama, and in Birmingham in what becomes known as the "Mother's Day Massacre." Six days later the Freedom Riders are beaten at the Montgomery bus station. The next evening First Baptist Church in Montgomery is besieged by a white mob. President Kennedy is forced to send U.S. marshals to disperse the mob.

1962   Representatives of SNCC, SCLC, CORE, and NAACP create the Council of Federated Organizations (COFO) to promote voter registration activities in Mississippi.

1963   APRIL–MAY. Massive protest demonstrations take place in Birmingham to challenge segregation. Led by Police Commissioner Eugene "Bull" Connor, the police attack protesters with dogs and fire hoses. Thousands are arrested, many of them children. So many thousands of children are involved that the campaign becomes known as "The Children's Crusade."

JUNE. Alabama Governor George Wallace tries to prevent integration of the University of

Alabama by standing in the doorway of the school.

JUNE. A group of civil rights activists, including Fannie Lou Hamer and Euvester Simpson, is jailed and beaten in Winona, Mississippi.

JUNE 12. Medgar Evers, the head of the NAACP in Mississippi, is murdered.

AUGUST 28. Over a quarter of a million people of all races join the March on Washington to demonstrate for civil rights. Martin Luther King, Jr. gives his "I Have a Dream" speech.

SEPTEMBER 15. Sixteenth Street Baptist Church in Birmingham is bombed. Four young black girls are killed in the explosion.

FALL. The Freedom Party organizes in Mississippi and conducts a Freedom Vote to show that blacks want to participate in elections, but are prevented from doing so by segregationists. More than 80,000 blacks vote in the Freedom election.

NOVEMBER 22. President John F. Kennedy is assassinated.

1964   SUMMER. The "Freedom Summer" project begins in Mississippi with a plan to bring more than a thousand young people to the state to work on voter registration and other community projects.

JUNE 16. Mount Zion Church in Longdale, Mississippi, is burned to the ground.

JUNE 21. Civil rights workers Michael Schwerner, James Earl Chaney, and Andrew Goodman, on a trip to investigate the burning of Mount Zion Church, are murdered by Ku Klux Klan members.

AUGUST 4. The bodies of Schwerner, Chaney, and Goodman are found buried in an earthen dam outside Philadelphia, Mississippi.

AUGUST. The Mississippi Freedom Democratic Party (MFDP) challenges the all-white state Democratic Party delegation at the National Democratic Party Convention in Atlantic City, New Jersey.

FALL. The first group of students integrates the schools in Montgomery, Alabama.

1965 FEBRUARY 18. Civil rights worker Jimmie Lee Jackson is beaten and shot by state police in Marion, Alabama. He dies eight days later.

MARCH 7. Civil rights demonstrators begin a march from Selma to Montgomery to protest the murder of Jimmie Lee Jackson and to demand voting rights for blacks. They are brutally beaten by police officers while crossing the Edmund Pettus Bridge in Selma. The attack becomes known as "Bloody Sunday."

MARCH 9. Reverend James Reeb, a Boston minister who had traveled to Selma to join the demonstrators, is viciously beaten by a white gang and dies two days later.

MARCH 21. Thousands begin a five-day march from Selma to Montgomery to demand voting rights.

MARCH 25. Viola Liuzzo is killed by Klansmen while driving demonstrators between Selma and Montgomery. She had come to Selma from Michigan to join the protest.

AUGUST 20. Jonathan Daniels, seminary student and civil rights activist, is shot and killed at point-blank range in Hayneville, Alabama. His killer is acquitted by an all-white jury.

AUGUST. President Lyndon Johnson signs into law the Voting Rights Act of 1965.

FALL. Thelma Eubanks and six other students integrate Gibson High School in McComb, Mississippi. Delores Boyd and Arlam Carr are part of a group that integrates Lanier High School in Montgomery, Alabama.

1968   APRIL 4. Martin Luther King, Jr. is assassinated in Memphis, Tennessee.

Who's Who

BOYD, DELORES: Montgomery, Alabama. At age eight, Delores started attending Montgomery Improvement Association (MIA) mass meetings. She says, "I grew up in those meetings, and I consider the MIA as much a part of my educational background as I do my formal schools. . . . That's when I got my excitement about being a lawyer. I remember Dr. King and others telling us about the legal battles. They'd say, 'Our lawyers are filing here' or 'Our lawyers are going to test this.' So it dawned on me early that the law played an important role." In 1965 she was one of the students who integrated the Montgomery schools. Today Delores Boyd is an attorney in Montgomery and co-owner of Roots and Wings, A Cultural Bookplace.

CARR, ARLAM: Montgomery, Alabama. Arlam was five years old when the bus boycott began. His mother had helped organize the MIA, and so he understood what was happening. "If we were driving and I'd see somebody walking, I'd say, 'Mama, Mama, pick those people up!'" When he reached high school age, he brought a lawsuit to end segregation in the Montgomery school system. Today he is a producer/director of a news program and other specials for Montgomery television station WSFA.

CARTER, MYRNA: Birmingham, Alabama. Myrna was arrested and jailed during the demonstrations in 1963. She says, "I was recently in church with my twelve-year-old son. Our pastor said we can look back and remember Reconstruction days. But rights were soon lost because we became too complacent. That disturbed my son. All the way home he kept saying, 'Mama, please explain it to me. Are they going to do to us like you used to tell me? Are we going to have to have certain water fountains again?'

" 'No,' I said. 'Of course there's room for improvement, but children don't have to use the side of the road for a restroom. They can go to any college they want to. The door is open. All you've got to do is apply.' " Today Myrna Carter Jackson works in retailing for a Birmingham department store.

CHANEY, BEN: Meridian, Mississippi. Ben was involved in civil rights activities with his older brother, James Earl Chaney, who was murdered by the Ku Klux Klan in 1964. Ben was arrested "more than twenty-one times before I was twelve years old" for "demonstrating without a permit." Today he is president of the James Earl Chaney Foundation, a human rights and civil rights organization. Among its projects, the foundation has been working to improve voter registration laws.

COLVIN, CLAUDETTE: Montgomery, Alabama. Claudette refused to give up her seat to a white person on a segregated bus nine months before Rosa Parks defied the same segregation laws. Claudette was fifteen years old at the time, and argued with the police officers that it was her "constitutional right" to remain in her seat. Her arrest and imprisonment were an early impetus for the boycott that was to be the beginning of the civil rights movement. Today she lives in New York City and is a nurse's aide at a private nursing home.

DEBERRY, ROY: Holly Springs, Mississippi. Roy grew up on a farm in rural Mississippi and attended a one-room schoolhouse. As a teenager, he became involved in the civil rights activities of the Student Nonviolent Coordinating Committee. In 1964, with other young people from the community, Roy wrote and performed in a play called "Seeds of Freedom" about the life and assassination of NAACP leader Medgar Evers. He asked, "Do you hate this white man for killing Medgar, or like a tree do you plant a seed of freedom and let it grow? In many ways in terms of symbols, we were the seeds, and so they didn't kill it." Today Roy DeBerry is assistant superintendent for education for the state of Mississippi.

EUBANKS, THELMA: McComb, Mississippi. Thelma was fifteen years old during Freedom Summer in 1964, and was arrested many times for civil rights activities. "Being a COFO kid made me feel like I was somebody, it really did. It just broadened our perspectives on things, letting us know we didn't have to take this if we didn't want to." She and several others were the first to integrate McComb High School in McComb, Mississippi. Today Thelma Eubanks Alston is a nurse's aide at an integrated nursing home in McComb.

FOSTER, FRANCES: Birmingham, Alabama. Frances was fourteen years old when she was arrested for participating in one of the first sit-ins in Birmingham. She remained involved through the 1960s. "I feel that the movement carries on with me today. I can do anything I want to do. I'm not frightened by anything or by anyone." Frances Foster White lives in Birmingham today and is a psychiatric technician working with adolescents at the University of Alabama hospital.

GADSON, MARY: Birmingham, Alabama. Mary was a teenager when she was involved in the 1963 Birmingham demonstrations. She says, "When we were growing up as blacks, you either were a teacher, nurse, or something like that. I didn't want to be any of those. To me, that was a stigma. I wanted to do something else, something different. And the movement gave me the sense that I could." Mary Gadson Russell married her high school boyfriend, Larry, also a participant in the Birmingham movement. Today she lives in Birmingham and works for a county agency, handling emergency food programs and running training workshops for volunteers.

GREEN, ERNEST: Little Rock, Arkansas. Ernest was one of the Little Rock Nine who integrated Central High School in 1957. He was the only senior in the group, and the first black student to graduate from

Central High. Ernest Green lives in Washington,
D.C. He was assistant secretary of labor for em-
ployment and training in President Carter's admin-
istration, and is currently an investment banker.

HENDRICKS, AUDREY FAYE: Birmingham, Alabama.
Audrey Faye was nine years old when she was
jailed for a week during the demonstrations in
1963. She says, "You always had a focus on why
you were marching. It meant to me a change. To
be able to go where we wanted to go. Not to be
traveling on the road and worrying can we stop
here, is this place okay? Not to have a fear that
you're driving into the wrong place at the wrong
time." Today Audrey Faye Hendricks lives in Birmingham and works for the Social Security Ad-
ministration.

HINKLE, TOWANNER: Selma, Alabama. Towanner
was a high school student when she marched in the
Selma demonstrations in 1965 to protest against
segregation and voting restrictions. She and other
students were arrested many times. When she herself reached voting age, she says, "the first place I
went was the courthouse. I was so proud to say I
want to register to vote." Today Towanner Hinkle
Grimes lives and works in Selma. She is also a
deputy registrar and works at the polls during elections.

HOWARD, BARBARA: Montgomery, Alabama. Barbara was six years old when she participated in the
bus boycott. She went on to become a teenage activist in the Montgomery movement during the
1960s. "I wish," she says, that "every child lived

in a home like the one I grew up in, with a mother who had the interest, the courage, and the foresight to raise children in spite of the odds, in spite of the poverty, in spite of the segregation, in spite of color. She never taught us to hate anybody, but to get out there and live life as if you are just as important as anybody else.'' Today Barbara Howard lives in Tuskegee, Alabama, and works at the Tuskegee Institute. She has also returned to school to finish up her college degree.

HOWARD, PRINCELLA: Montgomery, Alabama. Princella was a student leader in the Montgomery movement of the 1960s, heading the voter registration activities in 1964. The movement, she says, ''was my life. It was a real strong family. They were very strong, powerful cords. I mean, once you're in, you're in for life.'' Today Princella Howard Dixon lives in Jonesboro, Georgia, and is a marketing consultant for a health and fitness center.

JACKSON, JAWANA: Selma, Alabama. Martin Luther King, Jr. stayed at Jawana's house whenever he came to Selma. He was ''Uncle Martin'' to her. Jawana was four and a half years old at the time of the Selma movement in 1965, and recalls round-the-clock civil rights activities at Brown Chapel. ''I can remember going down to the mass meetings as a toddler. All the women frying the chicken, and the aroma of the food. You could get fed down there twenty-four hours a day, seven days a week during the height of the movement.'' Today Jawana Jackson lives in Atlanta, Georgia, and works at the Martin Luther King Center for Nonviolent Social Change.

LACEY, JOSEPH: Montgomery, Alabama. Joe was a teenage participant in the bus boycott. Toward the end of the boycott he drove a church station wagon, carrying people back and forth to mass meetings. He was frequently trailed by police but never caught. "I learned every little street in Montgomery so I could lose the police." Today Joseph Lacey lives in Montgomery and is the head of collections in the financial aid office at Alabama State University.

MARTIN, LARRY: Meridian, Mississippi. Larry grew up in Meridian and at age eleven was working at the civil rights center opened by Michael and Rita Schwerner. He says, "Freedom to me meant being treated equal. I mean, not just because I'm a black boy, but treating me right. That's all." Today Larry Martin lives in Meridian and works for a guitar company in the city.

PATTON, GWENDOLYN: Montgomery, Alabama. For Gwendolyn, "freedom meant that no one could say 'no' to me without a very good reason. I demanded a rational approach as a little child. It has kind of permeated my whole life." In college she became active in the Student Nonviolent Coordinating Committee (SNCC), participating in many protest actions to end segregation. Today Gwendolyn Patton lives and works in Montgomery. She helped organize the Alabama Democratic Conference to see how to "best utilize the black vote to have positive impact on the lives of our people." She continues to be a political activist.

ROBERSON, BERNITA: Birmingham, Alabama. Bernita was jailed with Dr. Martin Luther King, Jr. in the Birmingham protests in 1963. She was about ten years old, she says, when she began questioning the rules of segregation. "You grow up thinking you're second-class, that whites are superior. And I was one who just rebelled against that." After teaching for seventeen years, Bernita Roberson Sawyer now owns her own business, a travel agency in Atlanta, Georgia.

ROBERSON, JAMES: Birmingham, Alabama. James grew up across the street from the church and home of activist preacher Reverend Fred Shuttlesworth. "I was blessed to live then. I lived in a poor section of Birmingham, next to a church where a country minister began to say it's time for a change. I would not exchange the experience of living on that street corner and in that section for anything in the world. What most whites do not realize is that it was through the church that black people went to share the news, hear the word, and find out what was going on." In 1969 James became the first black salesman of Pontiac motor vehicles in the state of Alabama. Later, he was principal of a predominantly white school in Leeds, Alabama. After his retirement from the Alabama school system, he opened his own car dealership in Birmingham.

RUSSELL, LARRY: Birmingham, Alabama. When the civil rights movement began, Larry was a high school student. "I was ready. I had seen enough. I had questions that I wanted answers to. I got involved in the demonstrations by good old common sense, and being tired of the old stigma.'' Larry was jailed for ten days during the 1963 demonstrations. He lives in Birmingham with his wife, Mary Gadson Russell, and works for the telephone company.

SHUTTLESWORTH, FRED, JR.: Birmingham, Alabama. With his sisters Pat and Ricky, Fred participated in civil rights activities. The time he spent at the interracial Highlander camp in Tennessee had a powerful impact on him. ''I didn't realize how important it was for me to see folks from all over the world. We had not had experiences with white people until 1960. We had a chance to get to know that they're just like you, and that they play ball just like you do, sing like you do. There are a lot of black folk in the South who never had that experience.'' Fred went to jail with his sisters for refusing to sit in the back of the bus on the trip home from the Highlander camp. Today Fred Shuttlesworth, Jr. lives in Cincinnati, Ohio, and teaches ninth and eleventh grades and college freshmen.

SHUTTLESWORTH, PATRICIA: Birmingham, Alabama. Pat was fourteen years old when she and her sister Ricky tried to integrate Phillips High School in 1957. They and their parents were attacked by a white mob and prevented from entering the school. But this violence did not stop the Shuttlesworths' protest activities. Today Patricia Shuttlesworth Massengill lives in Cincinnati, Ohio, and teaches special education in elementary school.

SHUTTLESWORTH, RICKY: Birmingham, Alabama. Ricky was active in the Birmingham civil rights movement spearheaded by her father. She and her family survived a bomb attack on their home. "I was eleven years old when it happened. I heard a deafening sound, and then everything was blackened. I knew it was a bomb." But there were positive experiences as well. She felt "a part of something, a movement for change. I guess the movement made me want to help those who can't help themselves, those who can't speak." Today Ricky Shuttlesworth Bester lives in Cincinnati, Ohio, and teaches developmentally handicapped high school students.

SIMPSON, EUVESTER: Itta Bena, Mississippi. After high school, Euvester became a staff worker for SNCC. She believed that if blacks registered and voted and organized, "then maybe we could change some things. I didn't like the way things were, so I became a full-time SNCC worker. Being involved was probably the most important thing I've ever done in my whole life." Today Euvester Simpson Morris works as general manager for a management consulting firm in Columbus, Mississippi. She has also returned to college for a degree in political science.

STEELE, JOHN: Longdale, Mississippi. Michael Schwerner and James Chaney came to John's home when they were trying to set up civil rights programs in Neshoba County. They also came to his home when they were investigating the burning of Mount Zion, a black church in Longdale. It was to be the last day of their lives. Mickey Schwerner once told John that "freedom is worth dying for, fighting for other people's freedom." John says, "He made me see that freedom is not free. He paid the price for freedom." Today John Steele lives in Longdale, Mississippi.

TARVER, JUDY: Fairfield, Alabama. Judy was a senior at Fairfield High School, near Birmingham, when she was arrested and jailed for civil rights activities. She went away to attend college in Ohio. "When I came back and saw blacks driving buses, and the signs were down, I felt like I had something to do with it. I felt good about it. It's unreal how different it is. There are blacks *behind* the lunch counters. They're sitting *at* the lunch counters. I'm living on the same street that white people are living on. That would have been unheard of then." Today Judy Tarver Bostick is a medical technologist at a hospital in Birmingham.

TAYLOR, FRED: Montgomery, Alabama. Fred was thirteen years old when he participated in the bus boycott. "I remember people walking the streets. It made sense to me when I would hear Dr. King tell the story about this woman saying, 'My feet are tired, but my soul is rested.'" For Fred, "the movement gave me a sense of somebodyness. I was the first person in my immediate family to even finish high school. If the movement had not happened, I don't know where I would have ended up in life." Today Reverend Fred Taylor lives in Atlanta, Georgia, and is the coordinator of direct action—marching, picketing, civil disobedience—for the Southern Christian Leadership Conference nationwide.

WEBB, SHEYANN: Selma, Alabama. Sheyann was
eight years old when she became an activist. Her
involvement began when she saw a group of blacks
and whites "mingling together. That was unusual
to me. . . . I had never seen them in a friendly or
social environment where they were actually communicating." That was the first of many meetings
she attended. Within months she convinced her parents to go to a mass meeting, and for her ninth
birthday present she asked them to register to vote.
Sheyann was probably the youngest marcher on
"Bloody Sunday," when civil rights demonstrators
were beaten and teargassed by police officers. Today Sheyann Webb Christburg lives in Montgomery, Alabama, and is the owner of a public relations
firm that has developed cultural, social, and aca-
demic programs for young people. She and her husband also own a beauty salon.

WILLIAMS, GLADIS: Montgomery, Alabama. Gladis
was a teenage activist in Montgomery during the
1960s. She was thirteen when she and her sister
attempted to integrate a doctor's waiting room. She
says, "We used to hold workshops and talk about
the bus boycott, and how the movement started
here. We were determined to keep the fire burning.
The MIA was real important to us. We were young
folks, and we got our mind on freedom." Today
Gladis Williams lives in Montgomery and works
for the County Health Department as a home health
aide and emergency technician.

Acronyms

ACMHR	Alabama Christian Movement for Human Rights
COFO	Council of Federated Organizations
CORE	Congress of Racial Equality
MFDP	Mississippi Freedom Democratic Party
MIA	Montgomery Improvement Association
NAACP	National Association for the Advancement of Colored People
SCLC	Southern Christian Leadership Conference
SNCC	Student Nonviolent Coordinating Committee

Bibliographical Note

Although most of the material in this book is comprised of the words of the people interviewed, I prepared for the interviews by extensive reading of civil rights movement history and literature, and careful and repeated viewing of the splendid documentary series "Eyes on the Prize." Although all the books I read were instructive, several were steady reference sources:

Bates, Daisy. *The Long Shadow of Little Rock*. New York: David McKay, 1962; University of Arkansas Press, 1986.

Blaustein, Albert P., and Zangrando, Robert L., eds. *Civil Rights and the American Negro: A Documentary History*. New York: Washington Square Press, 1968.

Branch, Taylor. *Parting the Waters: America in the King Years* 1954–63. New York: Simon & Schuster, 1988.

Bullard, Sara, exec. ed. *Free At Last: A History of the Civil Rights Movement and Those Who Died in the Struggle*. Montgomery, AL: The Southern Poverty Law Center.

Cagin, Seth, and Dray, Philip. *We Are Not Afraid: The Story of Goodman, Schwerner, and Chaney and the Civil Rights Campaign for Mississippi.* New York: Macmillan, 1988; Bantam, 1989.

Garrow, David J. *Bearing the Cross: Martin Luther King, Jr., and the Southern Christian Leadership Conference.* New York: William Morrow, 1968.

————, ed. *The Montgomery Bus Boycott and the Women Who Started It: The Memoir of Jo Ann Gibson Robinson.* Knoxville: University of Tennessee Press, 1987.

Mendelsohn, Jack. *The Martyrs: 16 Who Gave Their Lives for Justice.* New York: Harper & Row, 1966.

Raines, Howell. *My Soul Is Rested: Movement Days in the Deep South Remembered.* New York: G. P. Putnam's Sons, 1977; Penguin, 1983.

Webb, Sheyann, and Nelson, Rachel West. *Selma, Lord, Selma: Girlhood Memories of the Civil-Rights Days*, as told to Frank Sikora. Tuscaloosa: University of Alabama Press, 1980.

Williams, Juan. *Eyes on the Prize: America's Civil Rights Years* 1954–1965. New York: Viking Penguin, 1987 (companion volume to *Eyes on the Prize*, the PBS documentary series produced by Blackside).

Index

Figures in italic refer to photo
  illustrations.
Additional photographs between
  pages 92 and 93.

Abernathy, Reverend Ralph, 20,
  32, 90, 162
ACMHR. *See* Alabama Christian
  Movement for Human Rights
  (ACMHR).
"Ain't Gonna Let Nobody Turn
  Me 'Round," 80, 103, 116, 152
Alabama Christian Movement for
  Human Rights (ACMHR), 71,
  94, 174
Alabama State College, 19, 30
Ambulances, 89
"America the Beautiful," 16
Arkansas State Press, 47
*Arlam Carr v. Montgomery County
  Board of Education*, 59–61
Arrests. *See* Jail/arrest
  experiences.
Assassinations. *See* Murders/
  killings/assassinations.

Baez, Joan, 146
Baker, Ella, 72
Baldwin, James, 114
Bates, Daisy, 47–48, 52
Bathrooms/restrooms, segregation
  of, 9, 12, 181

Belafonte, Harry, 146
Bennett, Tony, 146
Bethel Baptist Church,
  Birmingham, AL
    bombing of parsonage, 6–8,
  110
    Freedom Riders and, 87–88
    pastor. *See* Shuttlesworth,
  Reverend Fred.
Bevel, Reverend James, 144, 162
Billups, Reverend, 107
Birmingham, AL
    Bethel Baptist Church. *See*
  Bethel Baptist Church
    bombings, xii, 6–8, 71, 108–
  110, 154, 164, 175, 177, 189
    buses, 5–6
    Children's Crusade, 93–110,
  176
    Freedom Riders, 85–88, 176
    King, Dr. Martin Luther, Jr.,
  in, 94, 97, 99, 104–105
    marches/demonstrations/
  protests, 70–76, 93–110, 176,
  187
    mass meetings, 94, 99–102
    Mother's Day Massacre, 85,
  176
    police, 71, 76, 85, 93, 95–96,
  97, 98, 176
    segregation experiences, 13–
  17, 39–40

Birmingham, AL (*cont.*)
sit-ins, 183
Sixteenth Street Church. *See* Sixteenth Street Baptist Church. *See also* Carter, Myrna; Foster, Frances; Gadson, Mary; Hendricks, Audrey Faye; Roberson, Bernita; Roberson, James; Russell, Larry; Shuttlesworth, Fred, Jr.; Shuttlesworth, Patricia; Shuttlesworth, Ricky.
"Black is beautiful" slogan, 80–81
Bloody Sunday (March 7, 1965), xii, 144, 155–157, 178, 191
Bombings
Abernathy home and church, 20
Birmingham, AL, xii, 6–8, 71, 108–110, 154, 164, 175, 177, 189
Gaston Motel, 106
King home, 20
McComb, MS, churches, 10
Montgomery, AL, 20, 60
Nixon home, 20
Shuttlesworth home, 6–8, 110, 175, 189
Booker T. Washington High School, Montgomery, AL, 22–25, 29, 41
Boyd, Delores, 62–66, 147, 179, 180
Boyd, Henry, 40–41
Brotherhood of Sleeping Car Porters, 19, 108
Brown Chapel AME Church, Selma, AL, 144, 146, 149–154, 156, 157, 163, 185
Brown, Minniejean, 54–55. *See also* Little Rock Nine.
Brown v. Board of Education of Topeka, xii, 37–38, 47, 59, 173
Buses, xi–xii, 5–6
boycott. *See* Montgomery Bus Boycott.

Colvin, Claudette, and, 19–21, 25–28, 173, 182
Freedom Rides, 70, 85–92, 122–123, 176
Hamer/Simpson arrest, 133–135
interstate, 81–82, 85–86, 174
Shuttlesworth arrest, 81–82, 188

Carmichael, Stokely, 81, 139
Carr, Arlam, 59–62, 169–170, 179, 180–181
Carter, Myrna, 12–13, 39–40, 47, 104–107, 181
Carver, George Washington, 40, 48, 114
Carver High School, Montgomery, AL, 29
Cemeteries, segregation of, 1
Central High School, Little Rock, AR, 47–59, 175, 183–184
Chaney, Ben, viii, 3, 117, 120–127, 181
Chaney, James Earl, 114–115, 122, 125–131, 178, 181, 189
Children's Crusade, 93–110, 176
Churches
bombings. *See* Bombings.
burning. *See* Mount Zion Church burning.
segregation of, 1
white churches, 11–12, 72
See also specific churches.
Clark, Jim (Selma, AL, sheriff), 142, 149, 164–165
"Closed society" of Mississippi, 111–140
COFO. *See* Council of Federated Organizations (COFO).
Cole, Bud, 130
Cole, Jim, 128–129
Collins, Addie Mae, 108–110
Colvin, Claudette, 19–30, 38, 102, 173, 174, 182

Congress of Racial Equality (CORE)
  COFO forming, 113, 176
  Freedom Rides, 85, 176
Connor, Eugene "Bull" (Birmingham police commissioner), 71, 76, 80, 85, 93, 103–104, 106–107, 176
Constitution, U.S., 16, 27, 127–128
Corcroft, Freeman, 119–120
CORE. *See* Congress of Racial Equality (CORE).
Council of Federated Organizations (COFO)
  Eubanks, Thelma, 182
  forming of, 113, 176
  Freedom Summer, 113–115
  Meridian, MS, office, 116–119, 130
  voter rights projects, 113, 118
Cross burning, 10

Daniels, Jonathan, 154, 179
DeBerry, Roy, 8–10, 40–41, 136–140, 182
Democratic Party, 113, 133, 137–139, 178
Demonstrations. *See* Marches/demonstrations/protests.
Dexter Avenue Baptist Church, Montgomery, AL, 20, 23, 35. *See also* King, Dr. Martin Luther, Jr.
Disk jockeys, 101
"Dixie," 106
Doctors, 83, 191
Dodgers, the, 39–40
Drinking fountains. *See* Water fountains, segregation of.
Du Bois, W. E. B., 41

Eckford, Elizabeth, 48, 54–57. *See also* Little Rock Nine.
Edmund Petrus Bridge, 144, 156, 178

Eisenhower, President Dwight, 51, 52, 175
Eubanks, Thelma, 10–11, 66–69, 114, 168, 179, 183
Evers, Medgar, 120, 137, 177, 182
"Eyes on the Prize," 123

Fairfield, AL, 11–12, 97, 190. *See also* Tarver, Judy.
Farmer, James, 85
Fast, Howard, 114
Faubus, Orval (Arkansas governor), 47, 51, 53, 58, 175
Federal Bureau of Investigation (FBI)
  Connor, Eugene "Bull" (Birmingham police commissioner), report on, 85
  Schwerner, Chaney, and Goodman murders, 115, 131
  Selma-to-Montgomery march, 145
Fire hoses, 103, 107, 176
First Baptist Church, Montgomery, AL, 86, 89–91, 176
Foster, Frances, 74–76, 183
Foster, Marie, 163
Fountains. *See* Water fountains, segregation of; Soda fountains, segregation of.
Freedom Party. *See* Mississippi Freedom Democratic Party (MFDP).
Freedom Rides, *70*, 85–92, 122–123, 176
Freedom Road (book), 114
Freedom schools, 113–114, 123
Freedom songs. *See* Singing in; Songs.
Freedom Summer, 113–115, 120, 177, 182
Freedom Vote, 113, 177

Gadson, Mary, 30, 48–49, 74,
    102–104, 109–110, 147–148,
    183, 188
Gandhi, Mahatma, 80
Gaston Motel, 106
Gibson High School, McComb,
    MS, 66–69, 179
"Go Down, Moses," 103
"Go Tell It on the Mountain," 80
Goodman, Andrew, 114–115,
    120–122, 125, 130–131, 178
Gray, Fred, 28, 59
Green, Ernest, 43, 49–59, 175,
    183–184. *See also* Little Rock
    Nine.
Greensboro, NC, sit-ins, 71, 175
Greenwood, MS, 132–133, 135

Hamer, Fannie Lou, 133–135,
    138–139, 177
Hendricks, Audrey Faye, 94–96,
    109, 184
Henry, Aaron, 138
Highlander Folk School, 81–82,
    188
Hinkle, Towanner, 73, 163–166,
    184
Holly Springs, MS, 8–10, 40–41,
    136, 140, 182. *See also*
    DeBerry, Roy.
Horace Mann High School, Little
    Rock, AR, 49
Hospitals, segregation of, 1
Howard, Barbara, 34, 79–81, 148,
    184–185
Howard, Princella, 34–35, 142–
    143, 145–146, 185
Hrowbuski, Maggie, 39–40
Huntsville, AL, sit-ins, 77–79

"I Have a Dream" speech, 108,
    177
"I Wish I Was in Dixie," 106
Imprisonments. *See* Jail/arrest
    experiences.
Interstate buses, 81–82, 85–86, 174

Itta Bena, MS, 131–133, 189. *See
    also* Simpson, Euvester.

Jackson, Jawana, 159–163, 168–
    169, 185
Jackson, Jimmie Lee, 143–144,
    147, 154–155, 178
Jackson, MS, 86
Jail/arrest experiences
    Carter, Myrna, 106, 181
    Chaney, Ben, 117–118, 124–
    125, 181
    Children's Crusade, 94
    Colvin, Claudette, 19, 27–28,
    102, 173, 182
    Eubanks, Thelma, 182
    Foster, Frances, 76, 183
    Freedom Riders, 86
    Hamer, Fannie Lou, 133–
    135, 177
    Hendricks, Audrey Faye, 95–
    96, 184
    Hinkle, Towanner, 163–165,
    184
    King, Dr. Martin Luther, Jr.,
    99–100, 143, 187
    Martin, Larry, 117–118
    Roberson, Bernita, 99–100,
    187
    Russell, Larry, 101–102,
    187–188
    Shuttlesworth children, 82,
    188
    Simpson, Euvester, 133–135,
    177
    Tarver, Judy, 97–99, 190
    Williams, Gladis, 83–84
    See also Police.
James Earl Chaney Foundation,
    126–127, 181
Jewish children, 63–64
Johnson, Judge Frank M., 61
Johnson, June, 134
Johnson, President Lyndon
    Democratic Party Convention
    nomination, 138

phones Dr. Martin Luther
King, Jr., 162
  Selma-to-Montgomery march
protection, 144–145, 166
  Voting Rights Act of 1965,
144, 148–149, 179

Kennedy, President John F.
  assassination of, 177
  Freedom Rides, 89–90, 176
Kennedy, Robert (U.S. attorney
  general), 86
King, Coretta Scott, 169
King, Dr. Martin Luther, Jr.
  assassination of, 167–171,
179
  Birmingham, AL, in, 94, 97,
99, 104–105
  funeral of, *167*, 169–170
  ''I Have a Dream'' speech,
108, 177
  jailing of, 99–100, 143, 187
  Little Rock Nine, 58
  March on Washington
(August 28, 1963), 108, 177
  MIA president, 20, 174
  nonviolence, 73, 80, 104,
163
  SCLC president, 21, 175
  Selma, AL, in, 143, 144,
150–153, 157–163, 185
  speaking, 33, 84, 105, 108,
133, *141*, 167–168, 171, 177,
180, 190
KKK. *See* Ku Klux Klan (KKK).
Ku Klux Klan (KKK), 2, 10, 119
  King, Dr. Martin Luther, Jr.,
and, 161
  Liuzzo murder, 147–148, 179
  Schwerner/Chaney/Goodman
murders, 115, 178, 181

Lacey, Joseph, 30–32, 88–91, 186
Lanier High School, Montgomery,
  AL, 59–66, 179
Lawson, James, 73

Lee, Barbara, 67
Lee, Bernard, 162
Lee, Reverend George, 112, 173
Libraries, segregation of, 1, 72
Little Rock Nine, xii, *37*, 43, 47–
  59, 175, 183–184. *See also*
  Green, Ernest.
Liuzzo, Viola, 147–148, 154–155,
  165, 179
Longdale, MS, 115, 127–131,
  178, 189–190. *See also* Steele,
  John.
Lunch counters, segregation of,
  22, 71–72, 75–76, 83, *111*, 190.
  See also Restaurants; Stores.

Makarios, Archbishop, 160
Mann, Colonel Floyd (Alabama
  public safety director/state
  patrol head), 89
March on Washington (August
  28, 1963), 108, 177
Marches/demonstrations/protests
  Birmingham, AL, 70–76, 93–
  110, 176, 187
  bus boycott. *See*
  Montgomery Bus Boycott.
  Children's Crusade,
  Huntsville, AL, 93–110, 176
  March on Washington
(August 28, 1963), 108, 177
  Montgomery, AL, 4
  Selma, AL, 142–143, 153–
  154, 164, 184
  Selma-to-Montgomery. *See*
  Selma-to-Montgomery marches.
  Woolworth's, 71–72, 124
  See also Sit-ins.
Marion, AL, 143, 178
Martin, Larry, 116–122, 186
Mass meetings
  Birmingham, AL, 94, 99–102
  Freedom Riders and, 86, 92
  King, Martin Luther, Jr., at,
  33, 94, 104–105, 180
  Marion, AL, 143

Mass meetings (*cont.*)
  Mississippi, 10, 132
  Montgomery Bus Boycott,
    32–33, 186
  nonviolence training, 74
  Selma, AL, 152, 157–158,
    163–164, 185, 191
  whites at, 17
Mays, Benjamin, 160
McComb, MS
  church bombings, 10
  freedom schools, 114
  school integration, 66–69,
    179, 182–183
  See also Eubanks, Thelma.
McNair, Denise, 108–110
Meridian, MS, 3, 114–120, 130,
  186. *See also* Chaney, Ben;
  Martin, Larry.
MFDP. *See* Mississippi Freedom
  Democratic Party (MFDP).
MIA. *See* Montgomery
  Improvement Association (MIA).
Mississippi Freedom Democratic
  Party (MFDP), 113, 138–139,
  177, 178
Montgomery, AL, 3–4
  bombings, 20, 60
  Booker T. Washington High
    School teachers, 22–24, 41–42
  bus boycott. *See*
    Montgomery Bus Boycott.
  Freedom Riders in, 86, 88–
    91, 176
  marches to. *See* Selma-to-
    Montgomery marches.
  MIA. *See* Montgomery
    Improvement Association
    (MIA).
  school integration, 59–66, 178
  sit-ins, 72, 79–80
  See also Boyd, Delores;
  Carr, Arlam; Colvin, Claudette;
  Howard, Barbara; Howard,
  Princella; Lacey, Joseph;
  Patton, Gwendolyn; Taylor,

  Fred; Williams, Gladis.
Montgomery Bus Boycott, xii, *18*,
  18–21, 29–36, 174–175, 180,
  186, 190, 191
Montgomery Improvement
  Association (MIA)
  King, Dr. Martin Luther, Jr.,
  president of, 20, 174
    mass meetings, 180
    Montgomery Bus Boycott
  and, 20, 31, 34–35, 174, 191
    oratorical contest, 42
    organizing of, 20, 174
    Selma-to-Montgomery
  marches and, 145–146
    sit-ins, 79–82, 83
Moore, Margaret, 153, 155–156
Morehouse College, 160
Morgan, Charles, 108
Moses, Bob, 112
Mother's Day Massacre (May 14,
  1961), 85, 176
Mothershed, Thelma, 54–57. *See
  also* Little Rock Nine.
Mount Zion Church burning, 115,
  120, 128–131, 178, 189–190
Movie theaters, segregation of, 1,
  72, 79–80, 165
Murders/killings/assassinations
  Chaney, James Earl, 114–
  115, 121–122, 125–127, 130–
  131, 178, 181
  Daniels, Jonathan, 154–155,
  179
  Evers, Medgar, 120, 137,
  177, 182
  Goodman, Andrew, 114–115,
  121–122, 125, 130–131, 178
  Jackson, Jimmie Lee, 143–
  144, 147, 154–155, 178
  Kennedy, President John F.,
  177
  King, Dr. Martin Luther, Jr.,
  167–171, 179
  Lee, Reverend George, 112,
  173

Liuzzo, Viola, 147–148, 154–155, 179

Reeb, Reverend James, 147, 154–155, 179

Reeves, Jeremiah, 24–25, 34

Schwerner, Michael (Mickey), 114–115, 121–122, 125, 130–131, 178

Sixteenth Street Church bombing, 107–110, 177

Till, Emmett, xii, 9–10, 112, 137, 173–174

NAACP. *See* National Association for the Advancement of Colored People (NAACP).

Nash, Diane, 73, 86

Nashville Student Movement, 73, 86

National Association for the Advancement of Colored People (NAACP)

Alabama bans, 71, 174

Arkansas school integration, 47

COFO formation, 113, 176

Evers, Medgar, 120, 137, 177, 182

Howard, Princella, 145

Lee, Reverend George, 112, 173

Little Rock Nine and, *37*

Mississippi activities of, 112–113

Nixon, E. D., 19

Parks, Rosa, 19

Reeves, Jeremiah, 25

Neshoba County, MS, 115, 126, 189

New Pilgrim Church, Birmingham, AL, 94, 106

Nixon, E. D., 19–21, 28

Nonviolence, 73, 80, 104, 148, 163

"Northern interference," 105–106

"O Freedom," 80, 105

Orange, James, 142

"Outside agitators/troublemakers," 133, 136

Parker High School, Birmingham, AL, 43

Parks, Rosa, viii, 19–21, 28–30, 32, 174, 182

Parks, segregation of, 1

Pattillo, Melba, 54–57. *See also* Little Rock Nine.

Patton, Gwendolyn, viii, 3–4, 35–36, 48, 91–92, 186

Peck, Jim, 88

Philadelphia, MS, church burning. *See* Mount Zion Church burning.

Phillips High School, Birmingham, AL, 43–47, 175, 188

Police

Birmingham, AL, 71, 76, 85, 93, 95–96, 97, 98, 176

Corcroft arrest, 119–120

Freedom Riders and, 85, 89

Mann, Colonel Floyd (Alabama public safety director/state patrol head), 89

Marion, AL, 178

Meridian, MS, 115

Neshoba County, MS, 115, 126

Selma, AL, 142, 143, 144, 153–156, 164, 178

Winona, MS, 133–135

See also Jail/arrest experiences.

Ponder, Annell, 134

Price, Cecil Ray (Neshoba County deputy sheriff), 115, 126

Protests. *See* Marches/demonstrations/protests.

R. B. Hudson High School, Selma, AL, 163

Rainey, Lawrence (Neshoba County sheriff), 115, 126

Randolph, A. Philip, 108

Ray, Gloria, 54–57. *See also* Little Rock Nine.

Reeb, Reverend James, 147, 154–155, 179

Reese, Reverend, 165

Reeves, Jeremiah, 24–25, 28, 34

Restaurants/fast food, segregation of, 1, 13–14, 77–79. *See also* Lunch counters, segregation of

Restrooms/bathrooms, segregation of, 9, 12, 181

Roberson, Bernita, 99–101, 110, 187

Roberson, James, 4–8, 38–39, 46, 77–79, 87, 100, 187

Roberts, Terrence, 54–57. *See also* Little Rock Nine.

Robertson, Carole, 108–110

Robinson, Jackie, 39–40

Robinson, Jo Ann, 19–20, 29, 30

Russell, Larry, 14–17, 40, 73, 101–102, 183, 187–188

Rustin, Bayard, 108

Samuel Ullman High School, Birmingham, AL, 103, 109

Schools
Brown v. Board of Education of Topeka, xii, 37–38, 47, 59, 173
freedom schools, 113–114, 123
integration of, 38–39, 42–69, 173, 179, 183–184, 188
segregation of, xii, 1, 37–42, 47, 173
"Southern Manifesto," 174
See also Teachers; *specific schools.*

Schwerner, Michael (Mickey), 114–118, 120–123, 125–131, 178, 186, 189–190

Schwerner, Rita, 114, 116, 118, 123, 186

SCLC. *See* Southern Christian Leadership Conference (SCLC).

Segregation experiences, xi–xii, 1–17, 39–42, 83. *See also specific segregated facilities.*

Selma, AL
Brown Chapel Church. *See* Brown Chapel AME Church.
King, Dr. Martin Luther, Jr., 143, 144, 150–153, 157–163, 185
marches/demonstrations in, 142–143, 153–154, 164, 184
mass meetings, 152, 157–158, 163–164, 185, 191
police, 142, 143, 144, 153–156, 164, 178
Selma-to-Montgomery marches. *See* Selma-to-Montgomery marches.
teachers, 150, 153, 157, 163, 165
voter registration, 141–142, 150, 153, 158
See also Hinkle, Towanner; Jackson, Jawana; Webb, Sheyann.

Selma-to-Montgomery marches
"Bloody Sunday" (March 7, 1965), xii, 144, 155–157, 178, 191
second march (March 21–25, 1965), xii, 145–147, 158, 162, 165–166, 179

Shaw University, 72, 176

Shuttlesworth, Fred, Jr., 8, 46, 81–82, 188

Shuttlesworth, Mrs., 44–45

Shuttlesworth, Pat, 13–14, 42–47, 81–82, 175, 188

Shuttlesworth, Reverend Fred, 6–8, 43–47, 70–71, 75, 99, 110, 174, 188–189

Shuttlesworth, Ricky, 8, 14, 42–47, 72, 74–75, 81–82, 87–88, 175, 188–189

Simpson, Euvester, 112, 115, 131–136, 177, 189

Singing in
centers/meetings/workshops/church, 80, 90, 103, 116, 123, 152
demonstrations/marches, 95, 97, 106, 107, 124, 147, 153, 155, 164
jail, 82, 106, 135, 164
See also Songs.

Sit-ins
Birmingham, AL, 75–76, 183
Greensboro, NC, 71, 175
Huntsville, AL, 77–79
Meridian, MS, 117
Montgomery, AL, 72, 79–80
See also Marches/demonstrations/protests.

Sixteenth Street Baptist Church, Birmingham, AL, 94–95, 100, 101, 102, 105, 108–110, 177

Slavery, 11, 141, 160, 162

Smith, Lillian, 114

Smitherman, Joseph T., 164–165

SNCC. *See* Student Nonviolent Coordinating Committee (SNCC).

Soda fountains, segregation of, 4

Songs
"Ain't Gonna Let Nobody Turn Me 'Round," 80, 103, 116, 152
"America the Beautiful," 16
"Dixie," 106
"Eyes on the Prize," 123
"Go Down, Moses," 103
"Go Tell It on the Mountain," 80
"O Freedom," 80, 105
"We Shall Overcome," 80, 97, 116, 123, 144, 164
See also Singing.

Southern Christian Leadership Conference (SCLC)
Baker, Ella, 72
COFO formation, 113, 176
King, Dr. Martin Luther, Jr., president of, 21, 175
organizing of, 21, 175
Selma marches, 142–145
Taylor, Fred, 190

"Southern Manifesto," 38, 174

Steele, John, 127–131, 189–190

Stewart, Shelley, 101

Stores
Children's Crusade's effect on, 94
demonstrations/marches/sit-ins, 71–72, 83, 124, 143, 164
segregation in, 1, 4, 12–13, 22, 165

Strange Fruit (book), 114

Student Nonviolent Coordinating Committee (SNCC)
COFO formation, 113, 176
DeBerry, Roy, 136–138, 182
Huntsville, AL, sit-ins, 77–79
Moses, Bob, 112
organizing of, 72, 176
Patton, Gwendolyn, 186
Simpson, Euvester, 132–133, 189
voter registration, 132–133, 142

Sunday School bombing (Sixteenth Street Church, Birmingham, AL), 107–110, 177

Supreme Court, U.S.
Brown v. Board of Education of Topeka, xii, 37–38, 47, 59, 173
interstate bus ruling, 85
Montgomery bus decision, 33–34, 174–175

Swimming pools, segregation of, 72, 119–120

Tarver, Judy, 11–12, 96–99, 190
Taxicabs, segregation of, 1
Taylor, Fred, 32–34, 41–42, 72, 190
Teachers
　　Montgomery, AL, 23–24, 41–43, 62–66
　　Holly Springs, MS, 136
　　integrated schools, in, 62–67
　　Little Rock, AR, 54
　　McComb, MS, 66–67
　　segregated schools, in, 38–42
　　Selma, AL, 150, 153, 157, 163, 165
　　See also Schools; *specific schools.*
Telephone booths, segregation of, 2
Thomas, Jefferson, 54–57. *See also* Little Rock Nine.
Till, Emmett, xii, 9–10, 112, 137, 173–174
Train stations, segregation of, 5
Tubman, Harriet, 114
Tuskegee University, 48

University of Alabama, 48, 176–177

Vivian, Reverend C. T., 143
Voter registration
　　Chaney, Ben, 123, 126–127, 181
　　DeBerry, Roy, 136
　　Hinkle, Towanner, 166, 184
　　Howard, Princella, 185
　　James Earl Chaney
　　Foundation, 126–127, 181
　　Martin, Larry, 118
　　Mississippi, 112–113, 118, 123, 128, 132–133, 173, 176, 189

Selma, AL, 141–142, 150, 153, 158
　　Simpson, Euvester, 132–133, 189
　　Webb, Sheyann, 150, 153, 158, 191
Williams, Gladis, 84
　　See also Voting rights.
Voting rights
　　Selma-to-Montgomery
　　marches, 144–149, 179
　　See also Voter registration.
Voting Rights Act of 1965, xii, 144, 149, 179

Wallace, George (Alabama governor), 63, 80, 144, 176–177
Walls, Carlotta, 54–57. *See also* Little Rock Nine.
Washington, Booker T., 41, 48
Water fountains, segregation of, xi, 1, 9, 15, 21, 117, 181
"We Shall Overcome," 80, 97, 116, 123, 144, 164
Webb, Sheyann, *141*, 149–159, 170–171, 191
Wesley, Cynthia, 108–110
White churches, 11–12, 72
White, Paul, 101
Whitney, Eli, 114
Williams, Gladis, 82–84, 146–147, 191
Williams, Hosea, 150–152, 156
Winona, MS, 133–135, 177
Women's Political Council, 19
Woolworth's, 71–72, 124
Wright, Frankie, 116
Wright, Judy, 118
Wright, Richard, 114

Young, Reverend Andrew, 105, 162